Finding Our Way
The Saga of Georgetown College

Finding Our Way
The Saga of Georgetown College

Roger A. Ward
Forward by Rosemary Allen

RESOURCE *Publications* · Eugene, Oregon

Finding Our Way:
The Saga of Georgetown College

Copyright © 2025 Roger A. Ward. All rights reserved. Except for brief quotations in critical publications or reviews, no part of this book may be reproduced in any manner without prior written permission from the publisher. Write: Permissions, Wipf and Stock Publishers, 199 W. 8th Ave., Suite 3, Eugene, OR 97401.

Resource Publications

An Imprint of Wipf and Stock Publishers

199 W. 8th Ave., Suite 3

Eugene, OR 97401

www.wipfandstock.com

PAPERBACK ISBN: 979-8-3852-2321-3
HARDCOVER ISBN: 979-8-3852-2322-0
EBOOK ISBN: 979-8-3852-2323-7

For Eloise Felicity Strider and Julian James Ward Boyd

Table of Contents

List of Illustrations	ix
Forward	xi
Acknowledgments	xiii
Introduction	xvii

Part 1
Separation from the Kentucky Baptist Convention 1

   1. The Flagship College for Kentucky Baptists 3

   2. Liberal Arts and Academic Excellence
      by Karyn McKenzie 11

   3. Developments in Student Life and Sports 27

   4. Finances, Buildings, and Debt 35

   5. Crisis of Control in the Kentucky Baptist Convention 41

   6. New Directions for Georgetown College 47

Part 2
President Crouch and "the 27" 51

   7. Impact of the Separation
      from the Kentucky Baptist Convention 55

   8. Religious Life and Diversity 63

   9. Student Life, Greek Life, and Athletics 71

   10. Academic Programs and Faculty Hiring 77

11. Leadership Questions and Finances	85
12. Faculty Action and Its Result	91
13. Legacies of the Crouch Years	97

Part 3
Bright Hope for Tomorrow — 101

14. The Dwaine Greene Presidency	105
15. The Will Jones Presidency	117
16. A Woman for All Seasons: President Rosemary Allen	125
17. The Mission: Christian Service and Love by John Henkel	137

Epilogue: The Road Leads Ever Onward	161
Appendix: The Seal of Georgetown College	165
Endnotes	167
Index of Names	169
About the Author	175

List of Illustrations

Giddings Hall welcomes the morning sunshine	cover
Robert Mills presents presidential medallion to Bill Crouch	4
Alice (Gardner) and Bill Marshall are friends of GC	9
Doug Griggs receives Cawthorne Award	16
Students inducted into Phi Kappa Phi honor society	19
Bill Cronin encourages GC football team	32
Crowd gathers for Ensor Learning Resource Center dedication	36
Student newspaper headlines KBC vote to split with GC	45
GC students study at Regent's Park College, Oxford University	48
H. K. Kingkade presents for Christian Mission & Identity Task Force	61
Ralph Douglas West preaches at Bishop College Revival	64
Cynthia Insko is last co-funded Director of Campus Ministries	67
Brian Evans promotes Chris Briggs to head basketball coach	74
Sheila Klopfer is instrumental in review of faculty hiring policy	81
Martha Lane Collins represents GC	88
Students create logo to "Support the 27"	94
Jan and President Bill Crouch serve GC for 22 years	98
Carolyn and President Dwaine Greene join GC	107
Robyn Oldham receives recognition for long service to GC	110

Jonathan Sands Wise improves student enrollment and retention   112

Rosemary Allen is 26th President of GC   127

Robert Wilson and President Allen celebrate end of GC debt   135

The 8 Guiding Principles are displayed on campus   140

Gwen Curry is interpreter of GC mission   142

GC sign welcomes all to the college crescent and Giddings Hall   162

The images in this book are used by courtesy of the Georgetown College Archives. (c) Copyright by Georgetown College.

Forward

Rosemary Allen
President of Georgetown College

Georgetown College developed the plan for this book in the summer of 2022, when we were in a critical moment. An abrupt presidential transition had left the campus in need of a clear route forward in troubling times, and it seemed an appropriate time to assess the nature of our institutional journey.

With the financial support of the NetVUE grant program, "Reframing the Institutional Saga," members of the Georgetown College community under the leadership of Dr. Roger Ward collaborated on the research and writing of this book. The result incorporates many perspectives; it is the work of a community, for a community—a reflection on our shared past, and an assessment of our shared mission.

The volume focuses attention on the important accomplishments, challenges, and transitions of the past four decades, and how consequential decisions reshaped aspects of the institution. In reading this book, I was grateful for the opportunity to remember and relive the successes that moved this College forward; it is easy to forget the complex choices that made our College community what it is today.

We have experienced both difficult challenges and creative innovations over the past few decades, and the College of today is noticeably different from the College of 40 years ago. But we have remained true to a core sense of our historical mission, particularly our educational and religious mission. This book allows us to re-center our institutional self-perception so that we can move forward with a clear vision for the future.

As we prepare for the 200th anniversary of the College's founding, we should be heartened by the evidence this book provides of the College's commitment to thoughtful innovation, quality education, and spiritual development. As we plan for a bright future, we should be inspired by the past successes even as we take heed of the dangers that can face small colleges at every turn. Georgetown College's saga continues because it is a resilient and responsive community, committed to a shared mission. This book celebrates that community and mission.

Acknowledgments

This book is the result of a grant to Georgetown College from the Network for Vocation in Undergraduate Education (NetVUE), a program of the Council of Independent Colleges (CIC.) The vision of the NetVUE leadership in sponsoring a program for "reframing the institutional saga" was timely for our community. I owe special thanks to Director David S. Cunningham and Grant Director Carter Aikin for their expert support and guidance for this project, as well as to many others in the CIC who have benefited Georgetown College.

The fulfillment of this grant has been made possible by the administrative leadership of Georgetown College. President Rosemary Allen and Provost Jonathan Sands Wise actively supported the difficult process of institutional self-examination in evaluating College leadership and past decisions. Executive Assistants Jo Anna Fryman and Leah Stubbs provided invaluable assistance in recovering documents related to those decisions and facilitating conversations with individuals who knew the stories behind them.

I also owe deep thanks to the many faculty and staff colleagues, current and retired, who helped in this project, recovering memories and emails, and reading and commenting on sections. I am deeply grateful to John Henkel and Karyn McKenzie who not only authored chapters, but also provided helpful critical comments and insightful suggestions for revising the entire manuscript. Ed Smith ('88) was my primary partner in gathering the video interview material that formed the basis of the narrative. His perspective as a long-time faculty member of the College was a great support in the interview process. I will always recall the drive to Columbus, Ohio to interview Meda

(Banks) Mason ('57), one of the first Black students at the College. That interview became the basis of a Founders' Day Address. Among those who sat for interviews or provided answers to questions, I offer special thanks to William H. Crouch Jr., Hershael York, M. Dwaine Greene, Laura Owsley, Macy Wyatt, Garvel Kindrick, Alan Redditt, and Sheila Klopfer, who made a trip to Georgetown just for this project. I owe a debt of gratitude to Associate Vice President of Marketing and Communications Emily McCarthy for collecting the images used in this text and an accompanying website, and for creating the PowerPoint versions of this project for presentations.

I am also grateful to the College's Trustees who supported and added their voices to this project: Granetta Blevins, who has served in so many roles for the College, Guthrie True, Robert L. Mills Jr., and Earl Goode Jr., who made himself available for a crucial interview.

Three former colleagues played very important roles in the development of this project. Eric Fruge, a former Church Relations and institutional development officer, was instrumental in getting this work started. He opened his personal records and memories of the separation from the Kentucky Baptist Convention. Without his help that story would not be known in the way it is presented in this book. Robin Oldham, who served in the administrations of five College presidents, provided unique institutional knowledge and perspective that kept the narrative grounded in history. Robert Kruschwitz, my former department chair in philosophy, generously provided his expertise in designing the text and shepherding the book into publishable form. It was great to work together again!

Many of the interviews and conversations for this project happened at home and often in the evening. My wife, Elaine, has been my constant companion and supporter in this work, serving as a sounding board and a check on my interpretive framework. I owe her a debt of gratitude for her generous sharing of time and attention while I worked on this book.

Finally, to all who love Georgetown College and have found their way as students, faculty, staff, or just interested friends, this book is only possible because of your love and loyalty. This

Acknowledgments

community is held together by God's grace, seen in the long history of excellence, commitment, and sacrifice of so many people. May this book not only witness to the role Georgetown College has played in recent years but also deepen the role it continues to play in the ever-growing Kingdom of God.

Roger Ward

Introduction

Since its founding in 1829 by an organization of Baptist ministers, Georgetown College has become an admired liberal arts educational community, rooted in Christian love and service, that develops students who make a positive difference in the world. The College has changed as the needs of the community and higher education have evolved, facing external and internal challenges along the way. This project focuses on the story of the last 35 years of the College and three events that significantly impacted the College, culminating in the dramatic elimination of all institutional debt by President Rosemary Allen and 45 donors in 2024. The purpose of telling this story is to provide a record of these events and the people and decisions that enabled the College to survive and thrive through these years. But more than a guide to history or past events, this project aims to discover the driving character of Georgetown College that emerged from its Christian and Baptist identity, and how that character sustained it through three critical episodes. This narrative aims to describe the sense of mission or calling within the College that not only sustained it during its long history, but emerged with special meaning and direction in the recent times of stress. These events, considered from a narrative College perspective, support the conviction of the Spirit-led character that has distinguished Georgetown College's nearly 200-year history. We trust that character will provide continuing guidance for its future.

The first event was evaluating and ending the covenant relationship between the Kentucky Baptist Convention (KBC) and Georgetown College in 2005. Dr. William (Bill) Crouch Jr., the 23rd president, responded to the challenge from an organized movement of theologically conservative pastors, "Southern

Baptists for Kentucky," and the newly elected president of the KBC, Hershael York, in 2004. Concerns about the selection and control of College Trustees and faculty composition prompted Dr. Crouch to initiate the negotiations that eventually ended the College's affiliation with the KBC. This courageous step into independent status to secure academic freedom as a Christian liberal arts college marked the beginning of an era. The separation from the KBC heightened the significance for determining the College's institutional identity in the Baptist tradition of fidelity without creed. Many details of this event are recorded for the first time in this project. The consequences of this change continue to shape the College and its mission of providing academically excellent education in its Christian and Baptist context and tradition.

The second event was the forced departure of President Bill Crouch in 2012 at the urging of a group of faculty members. Following the separation from the KBC in 2005, the College's finances were stressed by the loss of the $1.2 million annual financial support from the KBC and a reduction of enrollment by students from Kentucky Baptist churches. Questions about the direction and leadership of the College arose on several occasions before the climactic expression of faculty concern and discontent in Fall 2012. At that time, 27 tenured faculty members sent a letter asking the Trustees to consider a change of presidential leadership. Board Chair Earl Goode ('62) met with these faculty in September and in early October Dr. Crouch announced his decision to resign as of May 2013. Crouch's leadership had elevated the College's profile while also protecting its academic freedom, but those accomplishments were shaded with continuing concerns about accreditation by the Southern Association of Colleges and Schools Commission on Colleges (SACSCOC) and the accumulation of a large institutional debt. The way forward was clearly going to be a challenge.

The third event was the termination of President Will Jones in 2021, and the appointment of Dr. Rosemary Allen as acting and then full President in 2022. Jones followed the presidency of Dr. M. Dwaine Greene (2013-2019) who responded to the College's need for a steady hand during turbulent financial conditions. Greene's spirit of humble service for the good of the College continues to resonate in the College's collective memory. Despite increases in enrollment and a balanced operating budget, the continuation of a SACSCOC sanction in 2017 stymied Greene's plans to enhance the College's finances by adding professional programs. Following Greene's retirement in 2019, Will Jones was selected as the 25th president and initiated a bold plan to quickly increase student enrollment. The outbreak of the COVID-19 pandemic interrupted this effort and caused the College to rapidly revise its policies on student housing and instruction. Jones experienced the stress of the growing financial challenges and exhibited behavior that led the Board of Trustees to remove him as president in October 2021, catching many people in the College community by surprise. They appointed long-time faculty member and Provost Dr. Rosemary Allen as Acting President in November 2021 and then President in 2022. Dr. Allen's long tenure of service as an English professor and Provost uniquely qualified her for the role, and the support from students, faculty and staff of her selection was overwhelming. In 2024, Dr. Allen, along with Trustees and friends of the College, completed a fundraising plan to eliminate $28.5 million of institutional debt accrued over the previous 30 years. This was the largest amount of money ever raised by the College. With the burden of debt removed, the College is now poised to focus on maintaining its health and responding to the current challenges of higher education.

Leadership and courage appear in different ways in this story: in the decision of a president to draw on Baptist principles of freedom to preserve academic independence of the College; in the grass-roots action of a group of faculty to speak collectively for a change of leadership; and in the wisdom of the Trustees to make a swift change and place the College in the hands of a service-minded leader who achieved the most positive fund-raising results in the College's history.

Behind these events, however, are the continuity and vibrancy of an academic community based on mutual trust and committed to its mission of Christian higher education. Proven academic leadership supported the educational excellence for which Georgetown is known. Despite challenges of financial duress and aging buildings, student life and religious life staff provided opportunities and experiences for students. Alumni and financial supporters of the College answered the call for resources. Long-serving staff in administrative and business offices maintained the operations of the College. These separate actions are bound together by a spirit of love and devotion, signs of God's presence invoked at Chapel services and at each faculty meeting. The College's communal commitment seeks to fulfill the phrase of a former professor that "God is in everything we do."

These reservoirs of work and sacrifice are the untold story that enabled the College to navigate these challenges. Taken together, these components of leadership and the fabric of dedicated support comprise the legacy of Georgetown College as it embarks on its third century, in which its people will continue "finding our way."

Part 1

Separation from the Kentucky Baptist Convention

When the Trustees selected Dr. William H. Crouch Jr. as the 23rd president in 1991, they were attracted to his vision that Georgetown College was "a diamond in the rough." He believed the college simply needed some polishing and exposure to be recognized throughout Kentucky—and nationally—for its excellence. Neither he nor they could have anticipated the impact of the changes Dr. Crouch would bring to the College, including the crucial importance of his bold decision to separate the College from the Kentucky Baptist Convention in 2005. That action marks a significant transition point in the College's history from a somewhat provincial but excellent denominational college into the broader landscape of a national Christian liberal arts institution.

Crouch was preceded by Dr. Morgan Patterson (1987-1991), a church historian who served at several Southern Baptist seminaries including Southern, New Orleans, and Golden Gate in San Francisco, California, immediately prior to coming to Georgetown as president. Although he fit the expectations for leadership of Georgetown in its role as the flagship college for Baptist liberal arts institutions in the state in the 1980s, significant changes were on the horizon. For one, in 1986, Toyota Manufacturing had selected Georgetown as the site for a factory that would eventually employ over 6,000 workers and bring profound population and economic changes to the area. Another change was the percolation of the conservative movement in the

Southern Baptist Convention into state conventions that impacted related institutions, such as Georgetown College.

Any effort to understand the context of the course adjustments that occurred during Dr. Crouch's presidency and to appreciate their impact on the College's identity deserves a more thorough review of Georgetown's history than space allows. So, rather than trying to paint the entire picture, we offer a few short, pertinent sketches.

First we briefly trace how Georgetown emerged as the flagship college for the Kentucky Baptist Convention, beginning with a key decision in 1958 to keep the College located in a rural community and focused on being an excellent residential institution. During this era the College developed closer ties with many KBC congregations. The next chapter, contributed by Karyn McKenzie, highlights the expansion of the academic programs within the liberal arts tradition. Then we sketch the growing importance of intercollegiate sports and the professionalization of student life services at the College. Finally, we consider how beneath these expansions of on-campus housing, academic programming, athletic competition, and student services were continuing struggles to gather adequate financial resources and consequently a deepening concern about institutional debt.

Chapter 1

The Flagship College for Kentucky Baptists

Georgetown College's history is deeply entwined with Kentucky Baptist history and life. All of its presidents were ministers until President Robert L. Mills, and the Board of Trustees was dominated by ministers, and its main alumni base was dominated by Baptist ministers and missionaries around the U.S. and the world. President Ben Elrod took on the task of completing the preparations started by Mills for the 150th anniversary celebration of Georgetown College in 1979. Dr. Mills' presidency (1959-1978) witnessed a long and stable period of growth, including the south campus residence halls, later named Mills Residence Park in his honor. A booklet commemorating the 150th anniversary highlighted the College's role in establishing Baptist higher education in the state and for Southern Baptists nationally. President Basil Manly Jr. (1871-1879), had been instrumental in bringing Southern Seminary from Greenville, South Carolina, to Louisville, Kentucky, in 1877. Georgetown College was founded primarily to educate Baptist ministers, and the path from the College to the seminary became a fixture for developing leadership in Kentucky Baptist churches. During the post-World War II era, Southern Baptists experienced a rapid expansion of membership and churches across America; in Kentucky alone there were more than 700,000 members in over 2,000 churches. Georgetown benefited from the confluence of a growing church constituency, government-sponsored tuition programs for returning military service members, and increased government investments in higher education. The campus expanded with new dormitories under Presidents H. Leo Eddleman (Knight and Anderson) and Robert Mills (South

Campus), fulfilling its role as the preeminent Baptist college in Kentucky. Despite the ever-present challenge of funding, Georgetown developed a reputation for academic excellence in religion, arts, music, education, and science. The College was considered a destination for higher education in Kentucky Baptist churches and families.

Georgetown College was central to the Kentucky Baptist vision for expanding higher education opportunities in the state. Perhaps the most significant event demonstrating its shaping role

President Emeritus Robert Mills presents the presidential medallion to Dr. William H. Crouch during his investiture in 1991.

in the development of Baptist higher education occurred in 1958. Under President Eddleman (1954-1959) the enrollment of the College doubled and Georgetown was in a building phase. The Eddlemans had been Southern Baptist missionaries to Palestine before returning to Louisville to pastor a leading church. Dr. Eddleman was also in close relationship with Southern Seminary leadership. A grand vision for Baptist higher education emerged from leading Baptists in Louisville that included relocating Georgetown to a site on Shelbyville Road in eastern Jefferson County and connecting the junior colleges of Campbellsville and Cumberland with Georgetown as branch campuses. The Kentucky Baptist Convention supported the plan, but the College's faculty opposed it. Two thousand residents of Scott

County signed a petition in opposition to the move. At a crucial meeting of the Board of Trustees held in Louisville, Senator John Sherman Cooper arrived from Washington, D.C., in time to cast the tying vote for the plan. The board chair, Dr. Richard VanHoose ('35), then cast the deciding vote against the plan, 16 to 15.[1] The College would remain in Georgetown. After the vote, several Trustees resigned, and Eddleman left to accept the presidency of New Orleans Baptist Seminary. Kentucky Southern College was established on the site intended for Georgetown in 1962, but it failed after a few years and its resources were acquired by the University of Louisville (Shelby Campus). Another result of this venture was that KBC granted the requests of Campbellsville and Cumberland to become four-year colleges. Thus, the landscape of three separate Baptist Colleges in Kentucky took shape from this event.

The Baptist community continued to seek ways to support the College and its educational mission. During the tenure of Robert L. Mills (1959-1978), a capital campaign was initiated by the KBC called Christian Education Advance (CEA). Although the $9 million program, of which 25% was apportioned to Georgetown, only raised a third of its goal, the KBC agreed to provide funds for repaying loans the College would need to build a science center and dormitories. The first major gift associated with the CEA was $650,000 by Lee Cralle of Louisville for the student center.[2] A survey conducted during this campaign revealed that of the 2,000 alumni respondents, 600 were ministers, with half serving in Kentucky. Additionally, it was found that Georgetown graduates had served as presidents of Baptist conventions in Alabama, Hawaii, Indiana, Ohio, and Kentucky.[3] A program of providing matching scholarships from Baptist churches and the KBC was created in 1972, which aided a significant number of Georgetown students.[4] Throughout this period choirs from the College regularly visited churches, and students formed worship teams and completed summer internships in churches with the support of religion faculty.

The College also relied upon its church constituency to address social concerns on campus. When Ben Elrod (1978-1983) assumed the president's role, he noticed a secularizing trend in student behavior. He asked the Campus Minister, Ira 'Doc' Birdwhistell ('68), to develop a plan to manage the campus culture toward Christian influences. Birdwhistell proposed the Pastor/Christian Leader Scholarship program, which allowed Baptist ministers to select two students from their congregations to attend Georgetown with a $500 yearly scholarship. Two half-tuition scholarships were awarded to outstanding students in this group. Classes of these scholarship students often represented a third of incoming students. In a few years, Birdwhistell noted, the campus culture had changed significantly due to the influence of these students, who assumed leadership roles in all campus organizations and clubs. These students also performed well academically and graduated at rates higher than other scholarship groups. This program continues today as the Christian Scholars program, the centerpiece of the Christian Leadership minor offered by the Religion department.

The Religion department broke new ground in the early 1990s by hiring the first woman as a professor in that department. Dr. Paul Redditt, an Old Testament scholar with degrees from Vanderbilt University and the University of Tübingen, Germany, had been hired as Chair of Religion in 1985 by Academic Dean Joe Lewis. Lewis knew Redditt when they were students at Southern Seminary and he valued Redditt's scholarly publications on Old Testament Prophets. When Dr. Vernon Mallow retired, Redditt and his colleague Dr. Joe Lunceford began to search for his replacement. Redditt says they were interested in hiring the best candidate, and if it turned out to be a woman, that was a plus. He and Lunceford were disaffected by the conservative movement within the SBC and wanted the College to "get with the times" by recognizing the value of women in religious education. After all, 55% of the students at Georgetown were women, many of whom were pursuing minors or majors in religion. Lydia Hoyle had moved to Lexington when her husband Rick took a position in psychology at the University of Kentucky. Lydia was finishing her Ph.D. dissertation in Church History at the University of North Carolina, Chapel Hill, and they chose the Lexington location over other options because there were a number of Christian liberal arts colleges nearby where she hoped to teach. Sharyn Dowd, a New Testament professor at Lexington Theological Seminary, met Lydia in a scholarship roundtable and recommended her to Redditt. Hoyle first filled in one course a semester in 1989-90 so that Redditt could work on a SACS report. She recalls grading final exams in the hospital after giving birth in December! She was hired full-time in 1991, the same year Bill Crouch became president. As the first woman teaching religion at Georgetown, Hoyle encouraged women students to pursue degrees in religion as well as careers in ministry. She also preached and conducted Bible studies for churches in the area, signifying the openness of the College to women in all roles in the academy and church life. Hoyle took a position at Campbell Divinity School in 2003 to be closer to family. She was replaced by Sheila Klopfer, who continued the support of women considering degrees and careers in religion and ministry.

Music education and performance also connected Georgetown to the Baptist community. Wayne Johnson formed an a cappella choir that frequently toured churches in Kentucky and surrounding states. The choir's excellence was renowned, and concerts in Hill Chapel were often at capacity with many local residents attending. The music department frequently had 100 majors and minors in its programs, including music education, instruments, voice, and directing. James Cordell ('66) led the 50-voice Baptist Student Union choir on church visits and out-of-state tours. He was selected as Director of the Worship Music Department of the KBC, where he served from 1985 to 2005. In that role, he supported full and part-time music ministers across the state with clinics and consulting, often using faculty from Georgetown. Danny Tilford ('57) regularly gave clinics in instrumental music at Ridgecrest, an encampment in North Carolina that drew members of Southern Baptist churches across the country. The integral connection of music and worship of the churches with graduates and students of Georgetown created a vibrant spirit of collaboration and education.

Throughout the 1980s and into the 2000s, approximately half to two-thirds of the students at Georgetown identified their religious affiliation as Baptist. Programming by campus ministry followed this tendency with large attendance at the Baptist

Student Union and leadership development. A program of mentoring support, Freshman Family Groups, was initiated by a campus ministry intern at the suggestion of Birdwhistell in 1992. This program offered 'family' groups of freshmen connected to 'parents' of students from higher classifications. Although a voluntary program, a large percentage of first-year students participated and moved into leadership positions for subsequent classes. The program functioned until 2017. The campus was also deeply influenced by the presence of Southern Baptist missionaries Ken and Beth (Stricker) Perkins from 1997 to 2000. Ken ('75 Religion and History) and Beth ('76 Education) came from the mission field on a leave of absence to recover from the death of their son. The "missionary house" on Main Street quickly became a locus of student gatherings, as Ken and Beth mentored students interested in missions. Even though Ken traveled weeks at a time gathering interviews for a book on persecuted people, groups of 40 students and sometimes 90 would meet for weekly meals and conversations. Justin Woods, Ben Crace, and Tim Miller were a few of the students who pursued mission work as a result of the Perkins' influence. Bill Crouch connected the Perkinses to a Trustee who funded their salary during these years and provided them with a home base for their ongoing work in missions.

The changing tone of Baptist life in the 1990s affected the role of Georgetown College in the life of churches as many evangelical Christians became suspicious of "liberalizing" influences of higher education. The conservative/fundamentalist movement within the Southern Baptist Convention raised the specter of liberalism in higher education, particularly with increased attention to biblical interpretation and theological content. The politics of the denomination may have been one of the reasons Birdwhistell transitioned to a position on the Religion Department faculty in 1997 after 18 years as Campus Minister. His devotion to developing the community of Kentucky Baptists was unparalleled in the state and was complemented by his historical interest, as reflected in his monograph, *Baptists of the Bluegrass: A History of the Elkhorn Association, 1785-1985* (Berea College Press, 1987). Birdwhistell proved to be a beloved minister and instructor to both students and faculty members. He mentored many students who felt a call to full-time ministry. Students could find him in his cluttered but comfortable office, where he often gave encouragement and guidance to future ministers who later served churches and organizations throughout the state of Kentucky. Following Birdwhistell, Sharon Felton was hired as Campus Minister. Since the position was co-funded by the KBC and Georgetown College it included reporting requirements and meetings with campus ministers from other college ministries in the state.

In 1998, Bill Crouch prompted the creation of the Marshall Center for Christian Ministry, a para-College organization with an assignment to develop Georgetown College's Christian mission.

Alice (Gardner) and Bill Marshall are leaders among Kentucky Baptists and good friends of Georgetown College.

The center was named for Bill ('57) and Alice (Gardner) Marshall ('57), Georgetown graduates who had served as Southern Baptist missionaries in Israel. After a decade working at the Foreign Mission Board as director of Human Resources, Bill Marshall became the executive secretary-treasurer of the KBC. From 1983 to 1997, he guided the convention to one of its most successful periods of church growth. In order to navigate the political tensions within the Southern Baptist Convention, Marshall led the convention in 1986 to establish "covenant agreements" with all the agencies of the KBC and its three affiliated Colleges. These agreements clarified the relationship with the convention and its role in Trustee selection in order to reduce the political anxiety caused by the conservative/fundamentalist movement in the Southern Baptist Convention.[5] The Marshall name and influence among Kentucky Baptists associated with Georgetown sent an unmistakable message of support, as did an initial gift of $500,000 for the center's endowment.

Another significant development was a $2 million grant from the Lilly Endowment awarded in 2000 to develop programs for the "theological exploration of vocation." Dr. Dwight Moody, Dean of the Chapel (1997-2008) and Philosophy professor Dr. Roger Ward (1996-Present) developed programs for students, faculty, and staff to explore their callings. With funding from the grant, students embarked on domestic and international mission trips, seminary visits, and religious retreats sponsored by Campus Ministry and by the Christian Leader Scholarship program. Although the form of programs and College leadership were changing, as well as the perception of the College's relationship within the Kentucky Baptist Convention, the College continued to provide excellent academic and leadership training for Kentucky Baptist students interested in ministry and religious vocations.

Chapter 2

Liberal Arts and Academic Excellence

By Karyn McKenzie

Although Georgetown College's identity has evolved over the decades, its academic core has remained grounded in the liberal arts and sciences. Georgetown College's reputation has historically been one of academic excellence within a Christian heritage, and this was certainly the case during the years 1985-2005. Faculty members strove to prepare students with the skills and knowledge needed to be successful throughout their undergraduate careers as well as after graduation.[6]

During the 1984-1991 presidency of W. Morgan Patterson, the College viewed its role as offering students "a community of rich tradition, high ideals, and academic excellence," while providing students with "a climate for achievement within a Christian context." Its purpose was to maintain "an institution of higher learning under Christian influences, historically related to the Kentucky Baptist Convention," and the yearly College catalog proudly described the institution's history as beginning with Baptist minister Elijah Craig's opening of a classical school. Outstanding academics within a faith-based environment was the Georgetown College way.

Beginning in 1987, College marketing materials said it offered "opportunities for excellence in intellectual, spiritual, cultural, social, and physical achievement within a Christian community." Thirteen goals of the College were added to its catalog, including that Georgetown would maintain a student body whose profile "remains above the national average within an atmosphere in which students of varying abilities can achieve to their fullest potential." College faculty had high standards for their students, and year after year, students generally lived up to those expectations. Although there were other Baptist and non-Baptist religiously-affiliated four-year schools in Kentucky, Georgetown typically enjoyed the reputation for being the most academically rigorous.

The arrival of President William H. Crouch Jr. in 1991 brought multiple changes to the way the College, including its academics, was perceived. For example, in 1992, Dr. Crouch introduced 8 Guiding Principles, considered the anchors of the institution. They were created to embody the values and spirit that "bond us as a caring community of students, faculty, administrators, and staff dedicated to recognizing and respecting the dignity and worth of each individual." The principles were Quality, Excellent Service, Loyalty, Teamwork, Positive Vision, Stewardship, Personal Growth, and Commitment. They were displayed on placards across the campus and they featured prominently in each course catalog between 1992 and 2001. Collaboration and loyalty were emphasized during campus presentations and faculty meetings. In this spirit, a fourteenth goal was added to the College catalog in 1990, promising to provide quality support services and facilities to strengthen togetherness. In 1993, the previous goal of offering continuing education programs was replaced with one emphasizing support for the larger community beyond the College by allowing access to cultural and athletic events, as well as offering the College's facilities and expertise. Campus attention was often focused on building relationships within and outside the College. Faculty responded to this emphasis by becoming more involved in the city of Georgetown, often through volunteer work. Simultaneously, faculty members were united with one another through their deeply-felt callings to be at the College.

Another change to the institution's identity occurred in 1995, when President Crouch developed the College's first-ever vision statement: "Georgetown College ... [is] an innovative community of scholars developing scholars committed to our heritage of Christian discernment." The College was to be a place where people of diverse backgrounds and lived experiences worked together harmoniously, creatively preparing tomorrow's leaders while permitting all campus members to pursue the truth. The vision statement was new, but its emphasis on scholarship and Christianity was consistent with the identity Georgetown had assumed since its inception. Later iterations of the vision included the phrase "scholars developing *ethical* scholars" (italics added). Georgetown was a place to learn and develop holistically, using principles of religious morality to inform one's decisions throughout life. To increase the likelihood of achieving the latter vision, President Crouch created a new cabinet position, Vice President for Leadership and Ethics. Dr. Judy Rogers was the only person to ever hold that role, from 1997 to 2004.

While a college president has authority over many aspects of campus life and personnel, at Georgetown College the faculty ultimately control the curriculum and are repeatedly espoused as the heart of the institution. When alumni share their most memorable or meaningful experiences from their time at the College, they often recount stories of specific faculty members who profoundly impacted their lives for the better.

There was a significant increase in the number of full-time faculty between 1985 and 2005. Approximately 70 full-time faculty members taught each year through the 1980's, before a dramatic increase in total faculty occurred during the late 1990's, when there were almost 90 full-time faculty. Faculty positions topped 100 in 2002 and remained close to that number through 2005. During this twenty-year period, most faculty were male, white, and had achieved the rank of full professor. Between 1985 and 1991, there typically were more than twice as many male as female faculty. From 1992 to 2005, on average, 62% of the faculty members were male. Faculty leadership roles were also predominantly held by males between 1985 and 2005, with 62% of division chairs across the College's five divisions being male. For almost half of those years, there was zero or only one female chair. Division chairs typically have limited power and decision-making authority, especially compared to department chairs. The gender statistics are even more disparate, however, when looking at this category. Across the existing 18-20 academic departments during this same time frame, only 28% of department chairs were female, compared to 72% male. The years 1998 and 1999 saw the highest number of departments led by women, with 44%. The lowest was the three years between 1988 and 1990, when only 12% were led by women.

Faculty arrived on campus with impressive educational credentials. While some faculty before 1985 graduated from top-tier schools, there were many more faculty with such pedigrees over the next 20 years. Faculty earned degrees from Duke, Harvard, Northwestern, Princeton, University of California at Berkeley, University of Chicago, University of Michigan, University of Pennsylvania, Vanderbilt, William & Mary, and Yale, among others. New faculty received their graduate programs' highest teaching and research awards while in graduate school. Many were interested in research, and they published articles, chapters, and books, somehow finding time to write and attend conferences despite heavy four-course teaching loads each semester and additional institutional and student relations duties. There was vibrancy among faculty members across campus, as they shared ideas, friendship, and academic interests. Faculty attended campus events, including co-curricular lectures and productions, as well as college-sponsored research talks open to the public. Campus was busy as faculty taught and supported students, conversed with one another, and remained committed to Georgetown's mission, goals, and vision.

The administration sought opportunities to acknowledge the skills, loyalty, and important contributions of the College's outstanding faculty members. For example, three endowed chairships were created to financially support faculty positions in different disciplines. In 1986, the Dwight M. Lindsay Professor of Biology endowed chair was established by Lindsay and his family, and a named scholarship was added in 1993. Dr. Lindsay was a revered faculty member who earned Emeritus status upon retirement in 1986. One year later, the James Graham Brown Professor of Business chairship began in 1987, after a donation by the James Graham Brown Foundation. Mr. Brown was a real estate developer and philanthropist who spent much of his life in Louisville. In 2003, the family of Marjorie Bauer Stafford ('37) established an Endowed Chair of Education in her name.

Stafford was a retired teacher for the Carroll County School System. All three of these chairships remain today.

In the late 1990's, education professor Dr. Douglas Griggs agreed to develop a faculty mentoring program for not only new faculty, but for all faculty interested in gathering with peers each week to discuss teaching. Under Griggs' guidance, faculty studied Parker Palmer's *The Courage to Teach* (1997) and met to discuss its relevance to their lives. Each week, Griggs described research-based teaching pedagogy studies and offered open-ended questions for group members to discuss regarding teaching techniques, student motivation levels, testing strategies, and personal teaching philosophies. He created a safe, nurturing, supportive environment in which faculty felt comfortable sharing thoughts about themselves and their peers. He assigned creative homework assignments that helped faculty focus on their calling to be effective, caring professors. In addition, he created schedules so faculty could observe one another in each others' classrooms and offer constructive feedback throughout the year. Many faculty still refer to their now slightly yellowed copy of *The Courage to Teach* because of all the insights it contains.

In a College-wide emphasis to recognize outstanding faculty, five faculty awards were established between 1988 and 2004. In 1988, Don ('31) and Chris Kerr Cawthorne ('33) created the Cawthorne Excellence in Teaching Award, which was first awarded in 1989. The Award is considered the highest honor bestowed upon a faculty member, as it is given to the nominee who best exemplifies across-the-board outstanding teaching techniques and student outcomes. Dr. Frank Wiseman, a long-time, beloved chemistry professor, was the first recipient.

Five years later, in 1993, Douglas Graves and Diane Graves Smith ('71) established the Rollie Graves Technology Excellence Award, in honor of their father. Each year, the recipient is a faculty member who best uses technology to enhance student learning, increase the joy of learning, apply classroom learning, and create innovative teaching methodologies. A staff member is also selected each year. Dr. Ilse Newbery, a German professor with nearly 30 years of experience, was the first recipient of this award, partly due to the success of her language laboratory.

The year 1997 brought the Marshall Center for Christian Ministry's Christian Service Awards, given to a faculty member, a staff member, and a graduating senior for their dedication to Christ and exemplary service in His name. Nominees were to live out the humility of Christ-like servanthood as well the courage and authenticity of the Christian faith every day. The faculty member named in 1997 was Dr. Bob Kruschwitz ('75), chair of the philosophy department, who served as a moral compass for many faculty members during his 21 years at Georgetown.

Douglas Griggs receives the 2010 Cawthorne Excellence in Teaching Award from Provost Rosemary Allen and President Bill Crouch.

Also in 1997, the John Walker Manning ('21) Distinguished Mentor and Teacher Award was created by Dr. Manning's widow, Mrs. Sylvia Beard. Those selected for this award have offered outstanding mentoring to students, received positive departmental evaluations and student evaluations, demonstrated collegiality, exemplified high moral character, and displayed Georgetown attitude and spirit. Dr. Douglas Griggs was the first recipient. He was selected in part because of the seemingly endless hours he spent with his students, encouraging them, listening to them, and helping them unravel the puzzle of the next phase in their life's journey.

The Lindsey Apple Student Life Appreciation Award was established in 2002 and named in honor of Dr. Lindsey Apple

Liberal Arts and Academic Excellence 17

('64) for his lifetime dedication to Georgetown students, both inside and outside the classroom. Recipients are recognized for their outstanding contributions to the co-curricular growth and development of their students. The inaugural recipient was psychology professor Dr. Karyn McKenzie for her work with Order of Omega and Psychology Bowl.

These awards and chairships show teaching excellence and student mentoring were hallmarks of the college. A primary reason many faculty members came to and stayed at Georgetown was the strong personal connections they felt toward students. It is to those beloved students this saga now turns.

Student enrollment steadily grew between 1985 and 2004. In 1985, Georgetown College had fewer than 1,000 full-time undergraduate students and approximately 150 full-time graduate students. But by 2004, these statistics had increased to 1,331 full-time undergraduates and 268 full-time graduate students. The average number of full-time undergraduates and graduate students during this 20-year period was 1177 and 130.

Most Georgetown students were Kentuckian, Baptist, Caucasian, and female. Between 1985 and 2004, approximately 80% of incoming students came from around 100 Kentucky counties, with Scott, Jefferson, and Fayette Counties being home for the majority of them. Graduate students represented approximately 30 Kentucky counties each year. Typically among the first-year students were some from approximately 20-25 other states, with Ohio and Indiana always providing the most. For the years data is available, 6 to 27 international students represented between 6 and 14 different countries. Anywhere from 45% to 62% of incoming students identified themselves as Baptist, followed by Christian, with Methodist and Catholic taking turns in third place. Each year about 7% of students stated they had no religious preference. Minority and international students consistently represented 5% of incoming students; most were African American, followed by those who were Hispanic, Asian, and Native American. There were always more females than males enrolled, as each year females made up anywhere between 52% and 58% of incoming students. Transfers accounted for between 28 and 62 additional students.

Between 1996 and 2005, the College created profiles of incoming students, including their academic statistics, participation in available sports, and financial aid packages. The ratio of students to faculty was 13:1 and the number of majors was 38 every year, while the percentage of faculty with Ph.D.'s increased from 80% in the late 1990's to 92% beginning in the 2000's. Incoming students' average ACT score hovered between 24.5 and 25, while their average high school grade point average was typically between 3.4 and just over 3.5. Student profiles revealed 87% of students received a combined $6.1 million in financial aid in 1996, whereas 96% of students received a combined $14.6-18.1 financial aid from 2001 to 2004. Georgetown College's finances appeared strong and were dedicated to improving students' success.

As Georgetown faculty members and administrators continued to emphasize academics, students benefited. A chapter of Phi Kappa Phi was created in 2003, the nation's 287th. Phi Kappa Phi is the oldest national honor society that recognizes academic achievement across all areas of study. To be a member, juniors' grade point averages must be in the top 7.5% of their class, while seniors' grade point averages must be in the top 10% of their class. Graduate students are also eligible for this prestigious organization.

In 2002, the College launched a new four-year Honors Program. Previously, students did not enter the Honors Program until the second semester of their junior year, and completion required three consecutive semesters of enrollment, focused on completing a thesis. The revised program required 15 hours (generally five classes) of Honors Credit Courses, an interdisciplinary Honors Seminar, and a three-hour Honors Thesis, for a total of 21 credit-hours of Honors coursework. All Honors courses except the Honors Seminar could count toward major, minor, or general education hours, depending on the courses selected. This fundamental revision laid the groundwork for future refinement of the Honors program to enhance the students' persistence in and completion of the program.

Ten students received Fulbright scholarships from 1991 to 2005, starting with Christina Schimmoeller ('91) who studied in

Liberal Arts and Academic Excellence

India, and ending with Michael Puglisi ('05), who completed his teaching assistantship in Germany. Other students received assistantships to work, teach, and research in South Korea, Belgium, Qatar, Spain, France, and Jordan.

Six-year graduation rates for Georgetown students, gathered from the Integrated Postsecondary Education Data System (IPEDS), averaged 55% between 1997 and 2005 with a high of 61.3% in 2004 and a low of 44.6% in 1999. The College graduated approximately 183 undergraduates each year between 1987 and 2006 (with missing data for six years), with 2004 boasting 256 graduates, and 1993 only 111. The five most popular majors between 1992-2004 were Business, Communication Arts, Psychology, Biology, and Education. Starting in 1995, Bachelor

Outstanding Juniors and Seniors are inducted into the Phi Kappa Phi Honor Society.

of Arts candidates outnumbered Bachelor of Science candidates, a pattern that remains today.

While there are some distinctions between BA and BS degrees, one common thread for all students is the set of graduation requirements they must meet. From 1987 these requirements have centered on the General Education curriculum, the major, the minor, and elective courses. In addition, there were logistical aspects: at least 128 total hours completed; a minimum of 2.0 for one's overall grade point average; a residency requirement that at least 30 of one's final 36 hours be earned through Georgetown coursework; at least 39 upper-level hours (courses numbered 300 or above); passing the comprehensive exam(s) for one's major(s); and attending a threshold of events in the co-curricular program. These six logistical aspects remained the same for the next 18 years.

In 1985, the College's General Education curriculum was comprised of seven areas of knowledge and human experience, allowing students considerable choice of coursework to meet the requirements while simultaneously introducing them to a wide range of thought, ideas, and content matter. The seven areas were Effective Communication (English and speech), Christian Faith & Values (religion), Natural Sciences (biological sciences, physical sciences, and mathematics), Cultural & Aesthetic Values (fine arts, and humanities), Foreign Language and Culture (French, German, Spanish, and Greek were offered in 1985; Latin was added in 1986; Japanese in 1996), Physical Education (activity courses), and Social Sciences (economics, political science, psychology, and sociology). The General Education curriculum was created to help students investigate relationships within and across the arts, humanities, natural sciences, and social sciences. Although many of the course offerings that satisfy each area have changed over the years, the core knowledge areas remain quite similar today. Although students were encouraged to complete their general education requirements during their first two years of study, this did not always occur. Each semester there were multiple first-year level courses with multiple graduating seniors enrolled, and this still occurs today.

In 1993, the faculty thoroughly considered the academic objectives they hoped all students would achieve as they completed their general education requirements. A year later, they endorsed six General Education goals, including effective writing and speaking skills, understanding the nature of Christian faith and religious values, awareness of varied methodologies used by natural and social scientists when conducting research, appreciation of the history of cultural values, understanding of a second language and culture, and appreciation of the connection between one's health and mind. In 1995, additional goals for the

Liberal Arts and Academic Excellence   21

General Education curriculum were established, shifting the emphasis from skills to whole-person development. Some of the new goals endorsed by faculty were "sound ethical values and heightened social conscience and responsibility," "an understanding and appreciation of diverse cultures and perspectives, both past and present," "experience in considering the fundamental questions of knowing oneself, the local and global community, the environment, and God," and "the desire and capacity for a life of continued physical, intellectual, and spiritual development." These goals remained almost unchanged for more than a decade.

During the 2003-2004 academic year, seven faculty members were appointed to the Revising Core Curriculum committee, tasked with thoroughly investigating the current curriculum and making thoughtful, timely suggestions for improving it. A year before she was named Provost, English Professor and Department Chair Rosemary Allen led the group. After lively discussions during multiple committee meetings and an on-campus winter retreat, the committee proposed multiple revision options to the full faculty. The changes supported by faculty fairly quickly related to total required hours and a new minor. The majority of faculty voted to decrease the total-hours requirement from 128 to 120, to allow students who completed an average of 15 hours each semester (rather than 16 hours each term) to graduate in exactly four years. In addition, faculty voted to approve a Liberal Arts minor, available to students who completed 15 upper-level hours across two or more departments outside of their major department. The third change did not have such an easy route to faculty support. For months, faculty meetings included heated, loud, and somewhat defensive debates as faculty considered where cuts in the general education curriculum should occur. Some wanted to require only one natural science course instead of two; others thought students needed only one social science course instead of two; still others thought the humanities sequence wasn't necessary, so long as students took one course in each of the three disciplines (history, philosophy, and literature). Some faculty members felt personally and professionally attacked. In the end, the sole change made to the core curriculum requirements was dropping the Kinesiology and Health Studies activity requirement, which reduced the general education hours by a mere one hour. All changes went into effect during the 2004-2005 academic year. Everything else related to curriculum requirements remained the same.

In 1985, students could choose from 33 majors and 15 minors. Eighteen department majors led to the Bachelor of Arts degree and 12 led to the Bachelor of Science degree. In addition, there were three interdisciplinary majors: American Studies, European Studies, and Environmental Science. Dual degree majors were offered in Medical Technology (until 2003) and in Engineering, and a Nursing Arts dual degree was added in 1987. The latter two dual degree programs continue today. Minors could be pursued in all academic departments, and in four interdisciplinary programs: Child Development, Family Studies, Social Studies, and Youth Ministries.

By 2005, there were 38 majors and approximately the same number of minors. Over the previous twenty years, most academic disciplines and majors did not change, but a few were added, altered, or removed. For example, the Home Economics major was cut in 1992, as was the Fashion Merchandising interdisciplinary minor. In 1996, the Health, Physical Education, and Recreation Department was renamed Kinesiology and Health Studies, and soon after that both the Recreation and the Physical Education majors were dropped. In 2004, the Communication Arts department split into two departments after faculty realized its two areas of instruction were no longer aligned in terms of a shared departmental mission or student outcomes. Communication and Media Studies joined the Social Sciences division, while Theatre and Performance Studies remained in the Fine Arts division. New minors were added in Women's Studies, Public Health, and Anthropology. New majors included Church Music, Commerce, Language and Culture, as well as Business Administration and Ethics.

As the world became more technologically-focused, faculty wanted their students to be prepared for its challenges and opportunities. In 1999, the College introduced a technology proficiency requirement for all graduates. Students could demonstrate proficiency during their first semester at Georgetown by successfully passing exams that assessed skills in using Word Perfect, PowerPoint, and Excel. Students who did not pass the exams could either attend relevant technology workshops and retake the exams, or successfully complete a one-hour course, Application Software. In 2003, achievement of technology proficiency no longer required students to pass exams; instead, it was enveloped into multiple general education courses, so students who successfully completed their general education coursework were credited with having demonstrated basic skills in using a computer and related information-technology resources.

Another cornerstone of the Georgetown College experience was its Co-Curricular program, created to emphasize liberal arts and sciences learning outside of the classroom, while cultivating students' aesthetic sensibilities. Students attended on-campus lectures, concerts, forums, dramatic presentations, and exhibitions. Some off-campus events might be included as well. In 1984, students were required to attend 12 co-curricular events from at least 50 offerings each semester, and their progress was noted on their transcripts. Attendance to twelve events was noted as a Pass, 10 or 11 events led to an Incomplete, and less than 10 events was noted as a Fail. Students who failed the co-curricular requirement two or more semesters were placed on academic probation and worked with the Academic Council to come up with a viable plan to get back on track. Any student with co-curricular deficiencies was able to get back in the College's good graces by completing additional coursework related to cultural content, although those courses did not count toward any other requirement, including total hours toward graduation.

In 1985, a streamlined program was renamed the Foust Co-Curricular Program (and later, Foust Co-Curricular Series), after partial endowment by Mary Louise Foust ('38) in memory of her parents, the Reverend David Taylor Foust and Margaret Rippel Foust. Students were still required to attend 12 events each semester, but now 35 instead of 50 events were offered. The transcript designations for completing the requirement and the opportunities to take culturally-based courses to compensate for less-than-ideal attendance remained. Four years later, in 1992, when the program was renamed The Foust Cultural Enrichment Program (CEP), the semester transcript designations were eliminated and the attendance requirement was cut in half. Students were now mandated to attend an average of only six events per semester they attended Georgetown, with no more than 48 required in total.

Beginning in 1992, Foust CEP events were classified into four groups: worship experiences, lectures, art/music/theatre events, and all other events. Students could receive up to 50% of their required credits from one group. Students who studied abroad received an event credit for each week they were abroad, up to 12 total. Some event speakers packed the Chapel, including Nobel Prize winner Eli Wiesel, former Presidential candidate Bob Dole, and former Secretary of State Madeleine Albright. Advisors were constantly reminded to discuss timely CEP event attendance during each registration meeting, so students would keep up with this requirement and not be burdened with attending an unwieldy number of events their last semester. Rumors circulated for years that students could pay cash to have event credits awarded to them by bribing Registrar Office personnel, but those were mere rumors. Deficits could only be made up through additional event attendance or coursework. The spirit and requirements of the CEP program remain in effect today with relatively minor revisions.

The combined quality of faculty, students, and liberal arts curriculum developed by the faculty led to a vibrant, academically-focused campus during the years 1985-2005. Faculty members were largely content with the College, students were discovering their interests and developing skills, and the administration was generally supportive of both faculty and students. During these years, Georgetown College was recognized by multiple national organizations and received the following distinctions: America's 100 Best College Buys; America's Best Christian Colleges; Barron's 300 Best Buys in College Education; A Best Southeastern College: The Princeton Review; Colleges of Distinction; Peterson's Competitive Colleges; Templeton Foundation Honor Roll of Character-

Building College; and U.S. News & World Report's Best Colleges. While the Southern Association of Colleges and Schools raised concerns related to finances, there were never any recommendations related to academic programs or faculty qualifications, which is rare. While there were occasional bumps of discontent along the way, in general Georgetown College academics were strong, students were motivated and engaged, and faculty remained energized and committed.

Chapter 3

Developments in Student Life and Sports

Georgetown College underwent significant developments in student life and sports beginning in the mid-1980s that dramatically reshaped the character of the student body. Student life benefited from the revitalization of intramural sports, the creation of new leadership programming for students, the institution of campus mental health counseling and career services, and the construction of the Center for Recreation. The College retained many of its traditions in Greek life and even added a new sorority, Alpha Gamma Delta.

Also during this era the College achieved notable and national success in women's and men's sports. Women's basketball and volleyball were regularly in national tournaments, and football won a national championship in 1991 followed by a national championship in men's basketball in 1996. As these successes elevated the profile of the College, the personnel searches for coaches and student life professionals attracted a broader range of candidates.

The notable expansion and professionalization of student life services began when Dr. Bert Hawkins ('67), a graduate of Georgetown who had joined the staff in 1978 as an assistant football coach, was named Vice President for Student Affairs in 1982. The position was later renamed Dean of Student Life. Hawkins, who also served as Athletic Director, established the Athletic Hall of Fame in 1998. With encouragement from President Crouch, Hawkins initiated the Harper Gatton Leadership Medallion program led by Melodie Fuller ('91).

Dr. Steve Bisese, a recent doctoral graduate from East Tennessee State, was hired as Dean of Men and later became

Dean of Students in 1999. Bisese brought extensive residence life experience at University of Richmond. A devout Catholic, he organized the Catholic Student Association, the first official non-Baptist religious organization on campus. Nearly a quarter of the student body identified as Catholic at that time. Bisese brought state-of-the-industry student life practices to the College. He began an international house that provided support for students of color and international students, and he contracted psychology professor Dr. Macy Wyatt to provide mental health counseling. He also added a program of career services for the first time at the College.

Perhaps the most important changes Bisese brought to the College were the people he hired. Melodie Fuller ('91), Laura Owsley ('92), James Koeppe ('95) Gretchen Lohman, and Charlene Lucas brought energy and new ideas to the student life and Greek life programs. As they gained experience and developed their skills, they continued their careers at other schools with several hired by Centre College in Danville, KY.

A significant shift in the culture of student life, with support from Dr. Crouch, concerned the approach to student conduct. For example, alcohol offenses were addressed with counseling and education rather than expulsion. Other organizational changes to student life were made in a spirit of experimentation and adaptation. Student Government Association (SGA) became Association of Georgetown Students (AGS) in 1993. Then AGS went back to SGA and created the Georgetown Activities Council (GAC). Student leadership was central in sponsoring events such as "Hanging of the Green" on the Sunday evening following Thanksgiving break. James Koeppe created a pre-college retreat called Directions in 2003 that engaged almost all incoming students in group-building and outdoor activities at the Tim Horton encampment in Campbellsville. This program continues today as the pre-college retreat for Christian Scholars students. Koeppe also led a leadership retreat for sophomores called IMPACT, and added an outdoor challenge course on East Campus in 1998 that operated until 2017.

The broad experience of the professional staff fostered other developments in student programming. For example, Steve

Developments in Student Life and Sports

Bisese played a role in the creation of one of Crouch's signature programs, The President's Ambassadors. When he interviewed Bisese, Crouch noticed that Bisese had been a President's Aide at William and Mary College. Drawing on research provided by Bisese about similar programs at other liberal arts colleges, Crouch began the President's Ambassadors in 1994. Twenty-three selected students worked as aides, driving the President's car to meetings, hosting visitors, and attending events representing the College. These students were trained in networking, etiquette, professional dress, leadership, and international travel. Selection as a President's Ambassador became highly competitive, and the cohort of PAs functioned as an informal link between the executive office of the College and the student body. The PAs received generous support for professional training and travel, often to European destinations.

The expansion of student life programs was fostered by a spirit of collaboration among Student Life, Academic Programs, and Admissions. Anne Leigh Bisese managed student financial aid and Gretchen Lohman moved into Academic Programs to work on initiatives to increase student retention. These relationships led to a combined effort to make Georgetown the best liberal arts college it could be, a private school but without a sense of elitism, according to Bisese. Students were proud to attend a private liberal arts college with willingness to try new programs without fear of failure. Bisese strongly advocated for building a recreation center for intramural sports and other student athletic activities. The building was completed on the site of the Hinton Field and named for George H. W. Bush in 2003. A multi-purpose room was named in Bisese's honor.

Dr. Todd Gambill served as Dean of Student Life from 2003 to 2013. He continued the professionalization of student life staff and was given additional responsibilities as Vice President over the physical plant, grounds, auxiliary services, and athletics. Religious Life was fully integrated with Student Life to provide more consistency and shared planning in programming related to students. Under Gambill's direction, mental health counseling services were established with the hiring of Dr. Ed Marshall, followed by Dr. Lloyd Clark and Megan Redditt.

Georgetown College's Greek organizations for men and women have been a vital aspect of student life for generations. There is a similar non-Greek organization, the Presidents House Association (PHA). These groups provide popular living settings for more than half the residential students and dominate campus culture with social gatherings, weeknight religious gatherings or "Devos," rush activities, philanthropic undertakings, and intramural sports competition. A highlight of the year is Song Fest, a program of musical skits performed during Homecoming. Carolyn Hale Cubbage ('71), Director of Student Activities, moved Song Fest from an outdoor performance on Giddings Lawn into the Chapel in 1988 or 1989. Song Fest became a focal point of Homecoming with the Chapel at capacity and fiercely competitive programs from the Greek organizations. Even the dress rehearsals for the show packed the Chapel.

Beginning in the late 1980s and going through the 1990s, the number of students involved in Greek societies nearly doubled. Recognizing the organizations as a force for enrollment and retention, Student Life supported them with a dedicated staff member and guidance on policies related to dorm rules and rush procedures. In recognition of the need for more opportunities for women in Greek life, Alpha Gamma Delta was added in 1999 and housed in the former Dudley Apartment building. A goal of the activities sponsored by Greek organizations was keeping students on campus over the weekends. Friendly competition on GPA comparisons served as encouragement for improving student academic performance.

The devotion of the alumni to these societies made them a backbone of financial support for the College as well as membership on the Board of Trustees. Greek organizations are the most significant cross-generational program at the College. Many alumni return to Homecoming for the purpose of reconnecting with their sorority and fraternity members. Composites of members from previous years populate the walls of the houses and are a deep source of pride and connection.

Georgetown College's athletic prowess during this era was particularly evident in men's basketball led by legendary coaches Bob Davis, Jim Reid ('70), and Happy Osborne. From the 1980s,

Developments in Student Life and Sports

women's sports emerged on the national stage in basketball and volleyball. Football developed into a nationally recognized program after winning a national title in 1991 and achieving success in the early 2000s. These achievements raised the College's profile, and sports camps for football and basketball attracted many prospective high school athletes to campus.

The football stadium and East Campus facility built in 1997 heightened media attention to these athletic accomplishments. President Crouch elevated the profile and competitive level of the College's athletic programs by developing personnel and increasing resources. The academic stature of the College aided athletic recruiting by stacking athletic and academic scholarships. Between 1987 and 2005, the College achieved three national titles and a score of Mid-South Championships. Standout individual athletes earned national recognition and awards, including Coaches of the Year in football, men's and women's basketball, and women's volleyball. Athletes as a percentage of the student body increased during this period, often approaching 45%. The attraction of sports participation provided strong support for the College's enrollment goals.

What follows are brief profiles of Georgetown College's most prominent intercollegiate athletic teams during this era.

Georgetown has a long history of basketball success. For instance, an alumnus Harry Lancaster ('32) served for 24 years as assistant coach to the legendary Adolph Rupp at the University of Kentucky. In the 1960s, athletics brought prominent Black students to campus, including Scottie Edwards ('68), who was recruited for football, basketball, and track. Edwards became the first African-American student to graduate from the College. Another remarkable event was alumnus Kenny Davis ('71) being chosen to captain the 1972 United States Men's Olympic Basketball team. The controversy of the Gold medal match with the USSR team led to the team rejecting the Silver Medals.[7] Basketball had long been the College's signature sport, especially during the career of coach Bob Davis. He was succeeded by Jim Reid who continued that success until his early death at 48 years of age in 1996. At the time, the team was ranked #1 in the NAIA and he was Coach of the Year. Happy Osborne, Reid's assistant, took over the head coaching job mid-season. The team went on to win the National Championship in 1998, and Osborne was honored as NAIA Coach of the Year in 1998. During this era the team won three Mid-South Conference Championships and competed in the National Tournament each year.

The football program was transformed by the hiring of Kevin Donley and Bill Cronin in 1982 from Anderson College in Indiana. In those days the football coaches also were responsible for another sport, tennis or track, and had classroom teaching

Coach Bill Cronin encourages the Georgetown College Tiger football team.

duties. Without the scholarships equivalent to those of its competitors, Georgetown won an NAIA National Championship in 1991, Bill Crouch's first year as President. Even though Crouch made it clear he wanted to move the football program to NCAA standards, the changes were not quick enough for Donley who left for a head coaching position in Pennsylvania. Crouch hired a new Athletic Director, Howard Pardue, who hired Bob Brush, the head coach of NCAA Division II Wofford College. After the team struggled for several seasons, however, Brush and Pardue left the College. Bill Cronin was re-hired as head coach for the 1997 season, and his first game was in the new stadium on East Campus, a site envisioned by Crouch as early as 1992. The stadium and facility were built to host the Cincinnati Bengals' training camp, and Cronin says the up-to-date facility and visibility of the Bengals helped him to recruit players. Between 1999 and 2002 the football team made the finals for National Championship each year and won titles in 2000 and 2001, with standout quarterback and three-time NAIA player of the year, Eddie Eviston ('02). The football Tigers were also Mid-South Conference Champions each year from 1998 to 2006.

Susan Johnson assumed the reins of the women's basketball program in 1978. She also coached volleyball and softball. Before Johnson the basketball team was led by several graduate assistants and had five different head coaches in seven years. This instability was quickly resolved with the hire of Johnson, who coached at Georgetown for 33 years. Her teams were Mid-South Conference Champions 2000, 2001, and 2003, and made it to the NAIA National Tournament eight times between 1989 and 2005. Johnson recalls the 2003 team as the one that put Georgetown on the map in the NAIA. With only six players in uniform they made it to the National Tournament, and three of the players earned All-American honors: Andi Johnson ('03), Neely Thomas Buhr ('05) and Rachel Vincent Salyer ('04). Johnson was voted Mid-South Coach of the Year from 2000 to 2005.

Donna Hawkins ('65) had been an exemplary student-athlete as an undergraduate student at Georgetown. She began her teaching and coaching career in 1980 and became the winningest coach in the history of the College. Her 73% overall winning percentage includes 560 wins in volleyball through 1997 and 309 wins in women's softball through 1994. Her 1997 volleyball team brought home championships from the Mid-South Conference and Mid-South Region Tournaments. She stands as one of the winningest volleyball coaches in the NAIA. Notable athletes from this time period include the Schimmoeller twins, Christina and Trina ('91), who led the volleyball team to its first appearance in the national tournament in 1988. They earned the Dean's Award and the President's Award at their graduation in 1991 and continue to engage in environmental activism through Kentucky Heartwood.

The success of these marquis sports programs aided the entire portfolio of athletics including tennis, soccer, baseball, and cross-country. Each of the coaches cited the College's superior academic reputation as a key factor in recruiting top athletes to their programs. By pursuing recruits with high academic credentials, they were able to combine academic and sports scholarships for more attractive packages of financial aid. As a result Georgetown earned a reputation for developing high-achieving scholar-athletes.

Chapter 4

Finances, Buildings, and Debt

When Bill Crouch became president of Georgetown College in 1991, no new buildings had been constructed on the campus since the 1970s. Presidents Elrod and Patterson had focused on stabilizing College finances and paying down the debt incurred with the construction of South Campus. During Patterson's administration, enrollment grew to 1600 students, the endowment doubled in value, and the College purchased a 50-acre farm east of campus. Pawling Hall was renovated with an elevator that provided access to its three floors. Giddings Hall was renovated and became the center for College administration. With no large building projects on the horizon, the College settled into an expectation of continuation but not growth. With President Patterson's retirement in 1991, the Trustees were interested in changing that expectation.

Bill Crouch was the most exciting candidate in the presidential search, according to Melodie Fuller, student representative on the search committee. Crouch presented a vision of what was possible at the College with new ideas and goals. The Trustees had voted to build a new library in 1972, but that project remained unfulfilled. At 40 years of age and with a keen attention to style, Crouch entered the landscape of Georgetown as a change agent. Though he was born in Louisville when his father was a student at Southern Seminary, Crouch's North Carolina accent and experience represented a very different feel as the leader of Kentucky-centric Georgetown.

One of Crouch's first actions was to borrow $4 million to spruce up the campus. With available assets of $20 million and a small but growing endowment, taking on this debt was not a huge stretch. The crescent sign on Giddings lawn was installed at this time. Crouch also engaged a design firm for a master plan of the campus that included a Learning Resource Center on Mulberry Street and a performing arts facility fronting Military Street. These two buildings would 'bookend' the campus. With this vision in hand, Crouch began the process of construction.

The Trustees set a goal for the amount of gifts in hand before beginning construction of a Learning Resource Center (LRC). Although this level of gifts and commitments was

A crowd gathers for the official dedication of the Ensor Learning Resource Center in 1998.

approached, it was not met when Crouch persuaded the board to begin construction funded from College resources. The Trustees were willing to take this step because the College had been so long without a new building they were anxious for some progress. An art building was added on the corner of Mulberry and College because the previous facility was demolished to make room for the LRC. Alumnus Robert Wilson ('62) gave $250,000 to name it for his wife, Anne Wright Wilson, as a birthday present. The Ruth Pierce Wilson Lab Theater also received an exterior renovation to match the new buildings.

A wrinkle occurred in 1996 when a College trustee familiar with the Cincinnati Bengals learned they were looking for a new practice facility. The Bengals had grown dissatisfied with the

Finances, Buildings, and Debt

campus of Wilmington College, Ohio, where they had been holding summer training camp. With encouragement from a group of supporters, Crouch developed a plan to build a stadium, conference facility, and apartments on the College-owned property east of the College. The challenge was the timeline. For the Bengals to commit, the stadium and complex had to be ready in one year. A plan to share the cost of the construction with the city of Georgetown was accepted, but a lawsuit filed by a citizen of Scott County challenged the deal due to the religious character of the College. Although the partnership idea was scrapped, the construction plan continued. With no time for fundraising, the College speculated that income from merchandise and parking related to the Bengals' training camp would offset the cost of construction. Reluctantly but resoundingly, the Trustees approved the plan. Construction began in 1996 and was completed for the Bengals' summer camp in July of 1997. The rapid construction timeline also meant that the ground was unable to properly settle before building began. Consequently, the stadium's lower level has experienced significant foundation cracking and water damage. Repairs are ongoing but will not resolve the problem of the foundation.

Another opportunity came from Bill Gillespie, a communications professor and manager of the College's campus radio station WRVG. At 500 watts, the signal barely reached the edge of the current campus. A request to the FCC to increase the wattage was answered with the news that a 50,000-watt channel had been reserved for that frequency, a signal equal to WUKY at the University of Kentucky and WHAS in Louisville. However, moving to that wattage would require expanded radio programming and professional staff rather than students. Gillespie's plan was for "World Radio: Public Radio Reinvented." With Crouch's support and the Trustees' backing, the College invested more than $2 million to build a station and hire professional radio personalities and staff.[8]

The president's residence on campus was also a source of concern. Built in the 1800s and modified in piecemeal fashion, it was not serviceable as either a residence or an event space. The Trustees approved a $500,000 renovation.

With the new football field and stadium on East Campus, the on-campus area of Hinton Field became available for other uses. Dean Bisese had reinvigorated intramural sports on campus, but Alumni Gymnasium could not accommodate intercollegiate sports activities, intramural games, and other student uses. With Bisese's advocacy a recreation center was proposed and approved, sited in close proximity to Alumni Gym with exercise machines and courts for basketball and other sports. Again, construction funds were provided by the College, although a plan developed to attract donations by naming the building for former U.S. President, George H. W. Bush. A naming ceremony was held but no donations emerged. The total cost of $5 million was added to the construction bonds held by the College.

The buildings and projects that were financed between 1996 and 2005 include:

- Ensor Learning Resource Center: $16.5 million
- Anne Wright Wilson Art Building: $3.3 million
- East Campus Facility: $20.8 million
- President's Residence renovation: $500,000
- Center for Recreation: $5 million
- WRVG: $2 million (sold for $1.7 million in 2004)

By 2003, the College's debt peaked at $43.8 million. With additional personnel required to manage these new facilities, the College experienced a budget shortfall for three consecutive years. This led to a cutback of 13 full-time positions in 2003. The loss of these employees shocked the College community and challenged the expansion mindset. Another consequence of the budget shortfall was the Trustees' decision to sell the radio station which had not generated financial support as expected. It was sold to K-LOVE for $1.7 million in 2004, and the tower remains on College property near the stadium, where it serves as a repeater station.

Crouch's previous experience in development and fundraising transformed the personnel and practices of Institutional Advancement at the College. After initial personnel changes, the team focused on cultivating established donors and

Finances, Buildings, and Debt

expanding contact with new donors. At Crouch's suggestion, the Trustees also created a Foundation Board as a vehicle for expanding donors among College alumni with significant wealth who did not meet the criteria for membership on the Board of Trustees. This focus on development activity successfully raised $95 million (restricted and unrestricted) over the 14-year period from 1991 to 2005. The total for Patterson's six-year tenure from 1986-1990 was $6 million.

Despite the fundraising success, increasing liabilities and interest payments on the bonded debt meant that the College's financial assets and tuition income were strained. The College's deficit budgets prompted the accrediting body SACS to place the College on probation for failure to comply with the standard of fiscal responsibility in 2004. This fiscal concern coincided with the change in the political climate within the Kentucky Baptist Convention, representing an external challenge to the already internally challenged institution.

In conclusion, the beautiful campus of Georgetown College and its academic reputation and sports success had led to a fresh vision of the College's character and possibilities. New buildings and programs expanded the campus and brought excitement of growth and development. Funding this growth had fallen principally to the Trustees and increasing bonded debt. The prospect of additional donors to the College to pay this debt and more students to fund the program with tuition dollars did not materialize as quickly as hoped. As the College entered the contest of control with the KBC, it was mindful of the approximately 5% of the annual operating budget provided by the Convention. In a curious way the debt may have helped the College in its negotiations with KBC because the denomination taking control of the College would also mean taking on its liabilities. This period of building expansion and rising expectations dramatically changed the perception of Georgetown College among its staff and faculty, as well as within the local community and among Kentucky Baptists.

Chapter 5

Crisis of Control in the Kentucky Baptist Convention

The relationship between Georgetown College and the Kentucky Baptist Convention was formalized in 1942. The KBC responded to the College's need for funding in the wake of enrollment decline due to the war effort. The mutual benefit was clear: the College served as a primary preparatory environment for education and leadership within the Baptist churches of the KBC. The College and the churches shared a consistent theological understanding of the world with the goal of developing their young people into thriving and faithful adults who would provide leadership for the churches in the future. Graduates of Georgetown became pastors and leaders in Baptist State Conventions beyond Kentucky, with many serving as domestic and international missionaries.

In 1976 a group of Southern Baptists organized a plan to take political control of the Southern Baptist Convention. This plan was called a "conservative resurgence" by its advocates and a "fundamentalist takeover" by its opponents. It split the Southern Baptist Convention (SBC), resulting in the dismissal of several seminary presidents and the disenfranchisement of a large number of former Southern Baptists. Roy Honeycutt, a long-serving and highly respected president of Southern Seminary, was replaced by Albert Mohler, just 30 years old and a partisan in the conservative movement. Southern Seminary was the destination for many of Georgetown's graduates pursuing careers in ministry and Christian higher education. Although Southern

Seminary was in the hands of the conservative movement, the churches comprising the Kentucky Baptist Convention remained largely free from denomination politics and most were decidedly moderate in theology. There was an uneasy relationship between the state convention and the seminary, and it was only a matter of time before the conflict would become a significant issue in Kentucky Baptist church life.

As the attention of SBC conservatives moved from the national organization to the states, similar conflicts emerged outside of Kentucky. The Baptist General Convention of Texas narrowly averted a vote to pursue legal action to prevent Baylor University from creating a self-perpetuating Board of Regents, effectively removing the university from the prospect of control by SBC leaders. In a similar manner Wake Forest successfully separated from North Carolina Baptists. William Crouch Sr., the father of Georgetown College President William Crouch Jr., was on the board of Wake Forest during that episode. Clearly, Bill Crouch was aware of the political landscape of Baptist politics when he became president of Georgetown College in 1991.

Kentucky Baptists had avoided political schism primarily through the efforts of Bill Marshall. He kept the national politics from affecting the fellowship of the KBC and worked to secure Georgetown's Christian character through the Marshall Center programming. Steve Cook ('73), Director of Church Relations, and Dr. Wayne Moore, Alumni Director, who had worked at the College since the 1980s, maintained long-term relationships with many Baptist churches and pastors across the state. With Moore's departure in 1995 and Cook's in 2001, however, these established connections were challenged. Dr. Eric Fruge ('75), supported by the Lilly-funded Meetinghouse programs, took over the role of Church Relations, which included directing the activities of the Marshall Center on campus.

In 2004, the political landscape of Kentucky Baptists shifted. In a surprising turn, Dr. Hershael York was elected president of the Kentucky Baptist Convention. Dr. York, in a pre-election interview, indicated that if elected president of the KBC, he would pursue the same goals as SBC leadership. York was raised at Ashland Avenue Baptist Church, an independent

Crisis of Control in the KBC

fundamentalist church in Lexington. Later as its pastor, he led the church to join the SBC after the conservative movement took shape. Educated at the University of Kentucky (BA, MA) and the Mid-America Reformed Seminary (MDiv, PhD), Dr. York was appointed Victor and Louise Lester Professor of Christian Preaching at Southern Seminary in 1999 by Albert Mohler. Five years later, York's election as president of the KBC in November 2004 marked the first time a conservative-fundamentalist candidate had achieved statewide office in the convention. The pattern in other state conventions was that a president would name people to boards and agencies who agreed with the conservative-fundamentalist plan for change. Because of the covenant agreement with Georgetown College, the KBC elected the members of the Board of Trustees of the College. With this power of elective control, the conservative forces would eventually come to dominate the College Board. The academic independence of Georgetown College was at stake. York and other conservatives expressed concern that their version of biblical inerrancy and fundamentalist theology were not represented in the Religion Department. They also questioned the teaching of evolution by science faculty. Thus, the election of York as president of the KBC raised deep concerns about the freedom to pursue scholarship, hire qualified faculty, and provide instruction to Georgetown College students without fear that certain topics or areas of inquiry would be stifled or curtailed due to perceived conflicts with a particular form of conservative Christian theology.

President Bill Crouch quickly mobilized College staff and Trustees to respond to the concerns resulting from York's election. Dr. Eric Fruge, Director of Church Relations and later a development officer at the College, was designated as the lead staff person to assist in formulating a successful response to the challenge. In the first months of 2005, Board of Trustees members engaged in tense discussions regarding how to respond to the election of York. At an off-campus gathering that included legal counsel, the Board decided to pursue legal separation from the KBC. The rationale for the decision supported the College's charter as a body independently organized and incorporated in

1829 that had voluntarily entered an agreement with the KBC after 1942 and formalized that agreement in 1986:

> On November 11, 1986, the College entered into a Covenant Agreement with the Kentucky Baptist Convention (the 'Convention'). This agreement provides for the Convention to annually elect the Board of Trustees. The Convention supports the mutual purposes of the College and the Convention by financial contributions to the College in accordance with recommendations as approved by the Executive Board of the Convention and by the Convention.[9]

Although the Trustees were elected by the KBC, the names put forward by the College were always accepted. This tacit agreement was now in question, with many concerned people wondering how the spirit of the covenant agreement could be modified or ended. Would the KBC require repayment of its funds, as occurred when Belmont University separated from the Tennessee Baptist Convention? Or would the KBC take Georgetown College to court to exert control over it?

During a fateful meeting in Frankfort in July, 2005, Trustee and lawyer J. Guthrie True ('81) presented the position of the College to a negotiating group appointed by the KBC's Education Committee. The College's position was to release the KBC from its financial obligation to the College and for Georgetown to remain a Baptist institution and select its own Trustees. After an extended private meeting, the KBC negotiators agreed to the terms. This decision would need to be ratified by the full convention meeting in November, 2005, and if that vote failed, the legal situation of the College would become much more difficult.

Bill Crouch and Eric Fruge spent the next several months traveling the state, speaking to churches, association meetings, and individuals to build support for the College's proposal. Fruge notes that the Warren Association meeting, organized and promoted by Dr. Jerry Oakley, the Director of Missions, was perhaps Crouch's most effective presentation to a doubtful or antagonistic group. Crouch made the case for the value of an

Crisis of Control in the KBC 45

independent Georgetown as a faithful Baptist and Christian College pursuing academic excellence and student development. As a result of this communication and contact, the November meeting of the KBC proceeded smoothly. York turned aside a parliamentary challenge to the motion as it was made, and he and Crouch stood together as the vote was taken. It passed overwhelmingly with more than 90% support.

In 2005, the Trustees approved the end of the covenant agreement with the KBC, effective January 1, 2006. Bill Crouch set three goals for the College going forward: to be a great Baptist College, to achieve Phi Beta Kappa standards academically, and to develop a $100 million endowment. These lofty goals were possible, Crouch believed, because financial assistance from

The student newspaper headlines the KBC vote to end its relationship with Georgetown College

donors and alumni would flow to the College now that the question of its independence from potential control by the KBC conservatives was settled. Fortunately, SACS removed the College from probation in December, 2005, so it began its new phase of institutional life without that encumbrance.

But questions about the impact of the change in relationship to the KBC and how it would affect student recruitment remained. Similarly, the separation from its main church constituency and the goodwill of Kentucky Baptists raised questions of where the College would find its place in the broader church landscape. What was its community now? Alumnus and pastor Alan Redditt ('00) noted that after the successful campaign to separate from the KBC, the College did not follow up with outreach or development of relationships with individual churches. In Redditt's opinion, this was an opportunity lost, one that would have long-term implications for the College. One reason for this lack of outreach was related to personnel. Eric Fruge was moved from Church Relations to Institutional Development, and his personal knowledge and years of relationships with KBC personnel and Directors of Missions were lost in that transition.

Beneath this turmoil of Baptist politics and negotiations about legal standing and relationships, Georgetown College was thriving in academics, religious life, student life, and athletics. The academic work of the College proceeded with clear signs of excellence: students studied in Oxford and other places around the world; the percentage of graduates admitted to advanced degrees or finding employment increased; the number of faculty increased. The early 2000s found Georgetown thriving and bustling. It was an exciting place to teach and be taught, as a student participating in athletics or Greek life or mission trips, or as a faculty or staff member confident that Georgetown was a stable and vibrant academic community fulfilling its mission.

Chapter 6

New Directions for Georgetown College

An outside observer of the events of 2005 between Georgetown College and the Kentucky Baptist Convention might conclude, with merit, that the events followed the pattern described in historian James Tunstead Burtchaell's book *The Dying of the Light: The Disengagement of Colleges and Universities from their Christian Churches* (Wm. B. Eerdmans, 1998). Burtchaell's thorough analysis demonstrates the difficulties of pursuing academic freedom as a motivation for resisting denominational controls on faculty hiring and curriculum development. While many fellow Baptist schools have severed ties with their denominations, several have rigorously pursued a Christian academic identity, including Baylor and Belmont Universities. Others, like Furman University, Mercer University, and the University of Richmond, have followed the secularizing path more distinctly. Georgetown College, as a liberal arts college with limited resources, does not fit easily into either category. The question of its direction following the separation from the Kentucky Baptist Convention falls somewhat outside the narrative Burtchaell presents. The separation was motivated by an intention to preserve academic integrity consistent with the core principles of Baptist polity that prize freedom from authoritarian control of the institution. In addition, the intention of remaining Baptist and Christian in character without formal connections to any denominational body placed Georgetown on a narrow path of success. How does the College resist the narrative of "outgrowing" its denominational origin and turn this dramatic organizational change into an opportunity for growth and exploration of new possibilities of liberal arts education?

How would the faculty change in relation to this institutional reorientation, led by their new Provost, Dr. Rosemary Allen?

A glimpse of a pathway emerged from the ad hoc collection of institutional relationships and programs that developed prior to the separation. The Marshall Center, with its independent board and funding, serves as a significant testament to the Baptist and Christian foundation of the College. Graduating students are presented with a Good News Bible, a translation made by College alum and missionary Dr. Robert Bratcher ('41). Awards for

Georgetown students Lindsey Kiser, Darren Burris, and Kevin Peacock study at Regent's Park College, Oxford University.

Christian leadership are presented to faculty, staff, and students during Baccalaureate services. The Christian Scholars Program, the largest scholarship group of students, was established with Lilly Endowment funds in 2001 under the direction of Dr. Roger Ward to include a comprehensive set of experiences from first year to graduation with requirements aimed at enhancing the students' sense of vocation. The vocation emphasis is expanded to all students by the Graves Center for Calling and Career. The Oxford program places high-achieving students at Regent's Park College, a permanent private hall at Oxford with a Baptist foundation, for credit-bearing tutorial courses. Faculty and pastors are also eligible for study-leave residence at Regent's Park. The two-course religion requirement for all students sustains the institutional commitment to academic study of the Bible and religion. Programs for developing the sense of Christian and academic vocation for faculty were also developed through Lilly grant activities. While these various efforts draw organically from the Baptist and Christian sensibilities of the administration, faculty, staff, and students, they were not constructed as replacements for a baseline institutional identity with a sponsoring constituency or denomination. Without a centralized plan, these programs function as expressions of religious sentiment or interest rather than exemplifying a core character of institutional identity.

In addition to the significant but fragmented programs related to Christian identity, the College was also newly cast upon its own resources and resourcefulness to secure its future viability. Although the KBC had not provided significant capital investment in Georgetown or its sister colleges for years, the regular financial support served as a symbol of endowment: it was a reliable source of income based on deep reserves of both fiscal and moral support. With the ending of the covenant agreement with the KBC, the College lost the denomination's backing in the present and the future. If the College were to face financial difficulties, the KBC would no longer be available to help or rescue it. This prospect of a future without a backing partner was most clearly evident in the 2004 probation by SACS following several years of deficit budgets and the staff reductions in 2003. The most threatening feature was the mountainous $43 million debt. The College had incurred this debt in part to provide an educational experience for future Baptist students, and now the pipeline of future students was in question. Academic freedom for the College, in terms of freedom from the threat of external fundamentalist control, was realized. However, this freedom now meant that the College leadership had full and sole responsibility for sustaining the community of scholars and the constituency that lent support and guidance to the College.

The questions that emerged following the separation from the KBC focused on the direction of investment and development that would best serve Georgetown College and secure its future. How was the College going to rally the resources to pursue this future? The fundraising success of the previous 14 years, while significant, was not well-managed. Bonded debt swelled and unrestricted net assets dwindled. The lack of financial discipline did not bode well for the College's immediate or long-term future. The main asset of the College was its history and reputation as an excellent liberal arts institution. Baptist identity and support had served the College for generations, and the primary standards of excellence were the expectations of Kentucky Baptists and its sister colleges. Crouch moved the sphere of comparison to regional and national liberal arts Colleges. The College did not fare well in these comparisons and rankings, based on stark differences in faculty pay, quality of residence halls, and investments in facilities. The comparisons magnified the disparities and fomented discontent. Athletics was clearly a bright spot for Georgetown, although the NAIA athletic conference compared the College primarily with denominational institutions, ranking it lower in national liberal arts standards. Each of these areas—finances, academics, residence life, and athletics—required a new formulation of direction and investment connected to the College's mission, even as that mission entered a time of reconsideration.

Part 2

President Crouch and "the 27"

Christian colleges and universities have had a profound influence in shaping American higher education. The life of the mind, moral integrity, and religious fidelity are woven into a richly varied tapestry of such institutions across the nation. But in the last half-century many of them have separated from their founding traditions due to the changing financial pressures of higher education, the shifting landscape of religious identity, the weakening of denominations, and the pressure to maintain academic reputation by hiring candidates who may not share or support those founding traditions. An impact of these changes—and Georgetown College fits well within this trend—is that institutions value leaders who negotiate institutional choices more with individual skill and cleverness than with insight into the principles and desires of a denominational community. With this shift to an independent leader from a denominational interpreter, to a person more akin to the CEO of a business than to a Director of Missions or a pastor of a congregation, also come new levels of evaluation from both internal and external perspectives. Bill Crouch's career after the separation from the Kentucky Baptist Convention is a clear example of this demand for a new kind of leadership for the College and the changing character of evaluation that leadership undergoes.

The dramatic conclusion of Georgetown's separation from the KBC, made official by a Board of Trustees action in January 2006, barely rippled the functioning of the College. Changes would come, but there was no event or ceremony to acknowledge this dramatic turning point in the College's story. Expectations of successful fundraising were high, and the rhetoric of Georgetown's uniqueness and focus on student success were energizing and captivating. College enrollment reached a high point from 2006 to 2009, buoying the hopes of institutional success for faculty and staff. Yet annual operating budget shortfalls were a regular occurrence and, in conjunction with the large institutional debt, fueled concern about the College's long-term financial viability.

Although President Crouch's leadership secured the academic independence of the College from the Kentucky Baptist Convention, the growth of financial resources needed to service the debt, develop the campus, and fund program expansion did not follow quickly enough. For instance, Crouch's often-stated goal of achieving Phi Beta Kappa standards appealed to the College's academic aspirations; however, due to the College's fiscal condition and administrative focus after 2005, this goal became increasingly unrealistic and was ultimately abandoned. The impact of the 2008 national financial crisis on Georgetown's finances and debt service dramatically impacted day-to-day operations. In 2009 eight promoted faculty were asked to forego their promised salary increases; though their salaries were later restored in the budget, this damaged faculty confidence. When student enrollment declined sharply following a change in Admissions Office personnel in 2010, this fueled the worries about the College's viability. To address these concerns, the Trustees engaged the Kaludis Consulting Group, which recommended the elimination of six majors including Music.

In late August, 2012, a group of faculty quietly organized and sent a signed letter to the Trustees advocating for a change in presidential leadership. Trustee Chair Earl Goode responded by agreeing to meet with the "27 faculty" who had signed the letter as well as the full faculty on September 29 to reassure them of Trustee attention to campus concerns. News of this action spread across campus and went viral on social media, raising the tension of the moment and increasing the attention of the wider College community. On October 2, Bill Crouch informed the College community that he was stepping down as president at the end of the academic year in May 2013.

President Crouch and "the 27"

The years leading up to this tumultuous event were marked by notable successes, standing against a background of concern about finances and College administrators' decisions. Success in football and basketball and other sports continued to attract athletes with excellent academic credentials. The faculty revised the general education curriculum, creating a common course model for all students, a first for the College. The Oxford program grew in popularity among high-achieving students.

Still, the question remained: what kind of Christian College was Georgetown going to be? At the behest of the Trustees, a task force led by H. K. Kingkade ('83) developed a Christian Identity statement that was adopted in 2012. At the same time, several faculty members challenged the Christian hiring practices of the College. After a multi-year study, a proposal was approved to open faculty hiring to non-Christians but it was not taken up by the Trustees. Despite the conflict among faculty, religious activities swelled with student-led groups on campus and international and domestic trips for service and mission supported by a Lilly grant and the Marshall Center. President Crouch initiated a focused diversity program in the Bishop Scholars. These markers of institutional success sustained and united the community of faculty, staff, and Trustees in the mission of achieving excellence as a Christian liberal arts college. They also served as a guide for action, leading to the difficult realization of the need to change presidential leadership.

Chapter 7

Impact of the Separation from the Kentucky Baptist Convention

The decision to separate Georgetown College from the Kentucky Baptist Convention, probably the most significant change to the College in its history, was made at the top levels of the institution, by the President and the Trustees. Faculty, staff, students, and other constituents were not included in the process or advised about the impact of the decision. In January 2006, the Board of Trustees formally acknowledged the end of the covenant agreement with the KBC, marking the beginning of its independent status.

The change from an organization affiliated with the Kentucky Baptist Convention to an independent organization that selects its own trustees and sets its own educational mission led to several profound changes. It marked a threshold event in the College's role as the leading educational institution for students preparing for preaching and music ministry in Kentucky Baptist churches. The number of religion majors declined, the students pursuing music majors to work in churches declined, and graduating students chose to continue their education at seminaries other than Southern Seminary, such as Duke Divinity School, McAfee School of Theology at Mercer University, George W. Truett Theological Seminary at Baylor University, and a start-up institution, the Baptist Seminary of Kentucky. The College's character as a training ground for "teachers and preachers" was replaced by focus on other professions. To retain the attention of prospective students and families, the College promoted itself as a leading liberal arts college with success in preparing graduates for business, the equine industry, medical school, and the humanities. The quest for additional revenue and student sources beyond the traditional Kentucky Baptist network led the College to entrepreneurial ventures, including the Global Scholars and the GC Vets programs which, while they were promising, did not generate the number of students or anticipated revenue it desperately needed.

The Trustees terminated the Covenant Agreement with the KBC effective January 1, 2006. The agreement established in 1987 included the formula of funding the College for two years at a time. A letter from the KBC Audit Group in February 2007 stated financial support from KBC to the College would phase out over the next four years. The KBC acknowledged the importance of the College for the Baptist community and encouraged them in that work. The absence of animosity in this transition, due to the KBC's decision not to pursue a legal challenge to the College's action, eased the transition. Bill Crouch affirmed to the KBC and to the public that Georgetown "would continue to be a great Baptist College, achieve the academic standards associated with Phi Beta Kappa, and develop a $100 million endowment." These lofty goals lifted the sights of the College community toward a hopeful and thriving future. Phi Beta Kappa standards were presented as early as 2001 as an aspirational goal when a committee of Phi Beta Kappa faculty of the College met to develop a plan toward achieving this target. That effort had stalled due to conflicts in approach, but the separation from denominational ties and the need for an aspirational academic goal to achieve these standards reignited that focus.

In October, 2006 the Trustees adopted a refined Vision for Georgetown College. They agreed that the College, both present and future,

- Must stand for Christianity
- Must be a place of superior academics
- Must become more and more distinctive
- Must move into the adult education market in a way consistent with its mission
- Must remain connected to the Church

Impact of the Separation from the KBC

The Trustees also dissolved the Foundation Board as of December 31, 2006. The function of the Foundation Board had been to gather alumni and friends of the College with financial resources who did not meet the requirements of religion and location to serve as Trustees. Since those requirements were no longer binding, the Foundation Board was not necessary. In a July 2006 meeting, the Board of Trustees amended its Articles of Incorporation to state that 75% of its members shall be Kentucky Baptists. The Articles of Incorporation were amended again around 2011 to remove the provision that any Trustee be a Kentucky Baptist, and add that a Trustee must be a "person of Christian faith and practice." Current Bylaws state that a Trustee have a "personal commitment to honor the Christian heritage of Georgetown College through active participation in a Christian congregation." The College's mission to maintain a connection to the church as a "great Baptist College" would require programmatic efforts other than Trustee composition.

Meanwhile, the loss of revenue from the KBC began to damage the operations of the College, but with little notice taken by those outside the administration. As the funding from the KBC decreased between 2006 and 2010, its impact on balancing the College's operating budget took on more significance. Even with increasing enrollment and revenue from tuition, the financial state of the College was constricted. The Trustees refinanced the bonds in 2006 with an aggregate principal not to exceed $42 million. The College also submitted to SACS a fifth-year follow-up monitoring report on short-term financial stability. Student housing was showing wear from delayed maintenance. Faculty and staff salaries did not increase, despite continued hiring to support the growing student enrollment.

The absence of overt conflict related to the separation from the KBC masked the informal and widespread shift of support by Kentucky Baptist pastors and churches away from the College. Since the 1960s, the College had developed strong connections with churches by promoting students visiting churches in choirs, worship teams, and ministry teams and for summer internships. From the 1980s, directors of alumni relations and church relations developed long-term connections with pastors and congregations; they facilitated student visits, spoke in individual congregations and at church association meetings, and held informal conversations with ministers and lay persons at convention meeting booths. With personnel departures in 1997 and 2001, respectively, the College's infrastructure of church connections began to shift, even before the 2005 separation. Dr. Eric Fruge replaced Steve Cook as Church Relations Director in 2001, and then H. K. Kingkade took over from Fruge in 2006. After 2005, the emphasis of church relations shifted to connecting with churches and pastors that supported the College. These churches largely identify with the Cooperative Baptist Fellowship, an organization formed as an alternative to the Southern Baptist Convention. Bob Fox, former minister of Faith Baptist Church in Georgetown, played an instrumental role in gathering church leaders to support the College during 2005. In 2018 he was selected as Coordinator of the Kentucky Baptist Fellowship, an organization of about 80 congregations in Kentucky that support the Cooperative Baptist Fellowship. In the years immediately after the separation, the bonds of connection with church constituencies began to reform along lines of affinity and a more progressive theological basis of church life.

Another feature of the separation from the KBC was changing lifestyle expectations and behavioral norms for students, faculty, and staff. For example, although there was no official policy against faculty drinking alcohol in public, it was widely understood that such practice was looked down on by the administration because it might offend the Baptist community. After the separation from the KBC, however, the hold of those previous norms was in doubt. For students, similar questions focused on the possibility of relaxed visitation policies to student housing of the opposite sex. Unlike most other liberal arts colleges, Georgetown did not have mixed gender dorms. And the question of the College's position in relation to the LGBTQ+ population emerged as a focus, especially for student life staff and faculty. Could students openly identify as gay or lesbian? Faculty were particularly aware of the vestiges of conservative Baptist mores, and they began to advocate for the development of policies and practices that reflected the general movement of

Impact of the Separation from the KBC 59

American culture toward acceptance and support on an inclusive campus. One student who enrolled in 2006 described it as an atmosphere of freedom and exploration, where students could sense that their behavior was no longer subjected to a conservative 'Baptist' standard.

Undergraduate enrollment had increased from 985 in 1985 to a high of 1,407 in 2006. Enrollment remained strong through 2009 and 2010 with more than 1,300 undergraduate students plus graduate students in education. This series of strong enrollments and good retention put pressure on the already stressed student housing. In 2008, every bed on campus was full, and the College had to locate students in hotels to accommodate them. Due to the close tie of the College's budget to enrollment, however, even small changes from expectations had profound impacts. A slight decline of enrollment from projections prompted decisions to restrict salaries of faculty, even as the goal of hiring new faculty to support Crouch's Phi Beta Kappa initiative continued. Stress on enrollment led to a change in 2009 when Johnnie Johnson was removed as Director of Admissions. Under the new director, however, the admissions office fragmented and enrollment significantly declined by 110 in 2010. By 2012, it had declined by more than 200 to 1088. This precipitous drop of more than 300 students affected every aspect of the College operation: student life, academics, and especially finances. During this period, the percentage of Baptist students also declined from 60% in 2005 to 38% in 2010, settling in the mid 30% after 2011. Hence, the impact of the separation from the KBC began to have significant consequences for the College, and these were further exacerbated by personnel changes made by the administration.

With the separation from the KBC, the historical character of Georgetown as a Baptist and Christian College came into question. The College relied on its connection to Baptists in Kentucky as a primary means of identifying its Christian character. The mission statements of the College from the 1930s identified it as a "Christian liberal arts College" working in relation with "the Baptist denomination in the state of Kentucky." Versions of the Christian and Baptist identity remained with some nuances in the decades that followed. In the

1950s College Catalogs, the College was described as educating with "Christian influence," in the 1960s as education in "a Christian context," and in 1986 as "under Christian influences." Because the separation from the KBC put more attention on this character, in 2010 the Trustees appointed a Study Group "to engage in conversations concerning the Christian Mission of Georgetown College." The charge, given to H. K. Kingkade, was to deliver a report to the April 2011 meeting of the Board of Trustees. Attention to the Christian mission was emboldened by the recovery of a long-neglected statement in the Bylaws of the Trustee handbook:

> The Christian mission of Georgetown College is to foster a knowledge of and commitment to the Christian faith. We will pursue this course as an institution committed to historic Baptist principles. The College encourages students and faculty to embrace their role in a community sharing God's redemptive grace for all people and traditions. The College's attention to intellectual honesty, integrity, and fidelity to faith in God helps men and women discern their many senses of Christian calling, including ministry, missions and service in the church as well as vocation in all chosen careers and fields. Georgetown College promotes academic excellence in its faculty and students as the means of discovering the truth about ourselves, our world, and God, integrating our heads, hands, and hearts to live active and productive lives following the example and teachings of Jesus Christ.

The existence of this statement was as a surprise to Kingkade. The Study Group, later named the Christian Mission and Identity Task Force (CMTF), that surveyed faculty, staff, students, and alumni about the College's Christian mission, included David Forman ('72), Jean Kiernan, Regan Lookadoo, Michael Rich, and Will Sampson. Their survey results showed a mixed perception of the value and expression of the Christian self-understanding. A report of initial findings delivered to the Trustees in April 2011, said that "a majority of faculty, staff, and students who responded to surveys reported that a Christian identity is important to them at Georgetown College." Among faculty respondents, 58% were committed to the College remaining a Christian institution and 23% were committed to maintaining its Baptist heritage. In response to the statement "The Christian mission and identity of Georgetown College is clearly communicated to the faculty," 14% strongly agreed and 13% strongly disagreed. The conclusion of the study was that "the Christian mission of the College remains vague."

Around the same time that the CMTF was meeting to discuss these findings and develop a common language about the Christian mission, three faculty members introduced a motion in the March 2010 faculty meeting to change the way Christianity

H. K. Kingkade leads an on-campus presentation of the Christian Mission and Identity Task Force.

was considered in faculty hiring. Diane Svarlien, a long-serving part-time faculty member, had decided to leave the College because her Jewish faith prevented her from becoming a full-time faculty member. In response to this, she and two other faculty members proposed a motion to replace the handbook language that "Georgetown College strives to be a Christian institution and expects its faculty to be Christian in fact and in behavior," with "Georgetown College strives to be a Christian institution and expects its faculty to support the Christian mission of the College and to exemplify Christian values in their behavior, providing effective role-models for students." The faculty referred this motion to the Faculty Committee. Its process of study and final recommendations will be described in Chapter 10.

Although this faculty-sponsored effort raised questions about the continuing nature of Georgetown as a Christian institution, the CMTF completed its work and produced a Christian Identity statement. After the statement was presented to the Trustees, Granetta Blevins ('80) requested a meeting with Kingkade to propose the inclusion of the clause, "Built on a Baptist Foundation." This was included in the final version that was submitted to the Trustees in December of 2011 and adopted in April 2012.

> Built on a Baptist Foundation, Georgetown College pursues and cultivates a knowledge of and commitment to the Christian faith. Faculty, staff, and students are called to embrace their role in our community characterized by God's redemptive grace for all people and traditions. Georgetown College promotes excellence to discover the truth about ourselves, our world, and God through integration of mind, body, and spirit. Committed to faith in God, the College encourages all to discern their mission and vocation to lead active and productive lives as exemplified in the teachings of Jesus Christ.

This statement continues to define the College's Christian identity on the website and in other College publications.

Chapter 8

Religious Life and Diversity

In many ways, especially with his education and previous experience as a Baptist minister, Bill Crouch cohered with the long tradition of Georgetown College presidents. The ethos of the campus and the tenor of the classrooms echoed this identity. For instance, several faculty members in the Religion Department and the Philosophy Department were engaged in conversations about Christian and Baptist higher education with other institutions, and the activities of the Lilly grant on the "theological exploration of vocation" extended those conversations broadly across the faculty. However, in the wake of separating from the Kentucky Baptist Convention, the faculty's investment in the religious identity of the College entered a time of reformation and revaluation. Without the demand to satisfy a sense of Baptist oversight, religious life programming was open to new forms and goals. And without a clear sense of direction from the administration about what the religious profile and practice of the College should aim to achieve, the religious dimension of the College, although vital and robust, began to show signs of susceptibility to fragmentation.

The chapel program at Georgetown College was the focal point for celebrating and expressing the institution's Christian mission. Worship services during the semester brought notable pastors and alumni serving in missions and other ministerial capacities into contact with students, faculty, and staff who attended. At the same time, student ministries were thriving with meetings and mission trips, and Greek organizations continued to sponsor their own regular worship services called "Devos" during the semester. The Christian Scholars Program fostered student interest in ministry and service by sponsoring domestic and international mission trips, as well as supporting student travel to explore seminaries for further study. The Marshall Center for Christian Ministry helped fund these trips and continued to offer preaching workshops for area pastors. Dr. Joel Gregory's influence led Dr. Crouch to initiate "Proclaimers Place," a preaching development conference for Black pastors who initially met at the College and later at Regents' Park College, Oxford. Many of these pastors were graduates of Bishop

Dr. Ralph Douglas West preaches at the Bishop College Revival at Georgetown Baptist Church.

College, which had closed in the 1980s. Crouch created the Bishop Scholars program to attract students from these churches, and further, succeeded in housing the records of Bishop College at Georgetown to provide a place its graduates could consider home. These actions jump-started the Office of Diversity, directed by Brian Evans, in 2006. The percentage of African-American students increased from less than 5% before the Bishop Scholars Program to 14%, a remarkable advance in only a few years. When Evans was named Vice President of Athletics in 2009, Robbi Barber succeeded him as Director of the Diversity and Bishop Scholars programs.

Another indication of the College's Christian and Baptist identity was the decision to host the Baptist Seminary of

Religious Life and Diversity

Kentucky (BSK) in offices and classrooms in the Ensor LRC in 2010. Dr. Greg Earwood, BSK's founding president, organized the seminary in 1996 in cooperation with the Kentucky Baptist Fellowship as a moderate Baptist theological response to Southern Seminary. Georgetown's hosting of BSK on campus clearly identified it with moderate Baptist theology and the Cooperative Baptist Fellowship. The Seminary and College shared a Registrar, Winnie Bratcher, and College faculty often taught classes for the seminary. Although they shared space and resources, such as library holdings, they maintained separate institutional structures and identities.

The developments of the religious life of the College, however, could not replace the impact of a coherent denominational identity and relationship to the large and geographically diverse community of churches of the KBC. The Kaludis consulting group noted in its 2012 report to the Trustees that the College's religious focus was neither fully nor clearly articulated, and hence its Christian character lacked the coherence and institutional effectiveness it needed for long-term success in that niche.

What follows are some snapshots of on-campus religious programming during this era: the chapel events and student ministries, and the various activities sponsored by the Meetinghouse, the Center for Christian Discernment, and The Marshall Center for Christian Ministry.

Soon after the separation from the KBC, Dr. Dwight Moody, Dean of the Chapel, organized a Ministry Reunion at the College in fall of 2006. More than 200 ministers and pastors affiliated with the College gathered for worship, fellowship, and seminars. The focus of the reunion was to re-center the College within the community of Baptist churches and ministers and to expand that community to churches of other denominations supportive of the College. High-profile speakers included Jim Somerville ('81) and Ken ('75) and Beth Perkins ('76). The reunion was a reminder of the rich educational legacy of Georgetown College and its impact on the lives and work of many pastors over several generations. Moody resigned from his position as Dean of the Chapel in 2009 due to conflicts with the administration and budget pressure. The position was not rehired, and H. K Kingkade took leadership of church relations and served as Director of Religious Life before moving to Marketing and later, to Admissions.

Campus Ministry was led by Cynthia Insko. Her position, co-funded by the Kentucky Baptist Convention and Georgetown College, was a vestige of the financial partnership between the Convention and the College after their separation. In 2006, Bryan Langlands, an ordained United Methodist minister, was hired as Associate Campus Minister. Under Insko's leadership, programs supporting women interested in ministry were added. The KBC ended their support of the campus minister position in 2010, and Insko was succeeded by Langlands. During these years, multiple collegiate ministries served on campus. Campus Ministry, the name of the former Baptist Student Union, included several student ministries under its umbrella: the Chapel ministry, Freshmen Family Groups (a small-group ministry for first year students led by older students), Common Ground (a weekly student-led worship service), Scroggins Park (a weekly after-school mentoring and tutoring program in a low-income neighborhood in Georgetown), and various student-led ministries with low-income folks in Georgetown (partnering with the Gathering Place mission) and in downtown Lexington. Other collegiate ministries began during this time, including the Newman Center (a Catholic student ministry), Fellowship of Christian Athletes (FCA), and Campus Outreach (a campus organization sponsored by the Presbyterian Church of America). Collectively, these ministries drew significant numbers of students to weekly meetings and attracted several students into collegiate ministry leadership on other campuses after graduation. Among these were Shea James ('07), Tara Jo Sword Crawford ('12), Jimmy Lacy, and Sean Schweickhardt ('08). On a regular basis, Langlands gathered the student leaders from the different ministries for lunches, relationship-building, prayer, and Christian leadership coaching. At least once or twice a year all the ministries would cancel their regularly scheduled meetings to join together for an all-campus unity worship service, which was often held during Holy Week.

Langlands taught almost all the ministry classes in the Religion Department and helped to start a ministry studies track within the religion major. He was involved in the College's Quality Enhancement Program (QEP) that focused on increasing the number of students who participated in service learning. As a result, most of the ministry classes Langlands taught included a service-learning component, where students gained required field experience by serving with and learning from local churches. Many students were influenced by opportunities to minister with local congregations through these local church connections and they continued their education to seminary. Mary Alice Birdwhistell ('09), Michelle Ballard ('14), Marcus Price ('19), and Jose Baeza ('14) were notable students from this era.

Cynthia Insko is the last Director of Campus Ministries co-funded by the Kentucky Baptist Convention and Georgetown College.

Based on the success of the programs and activities funded by the $2 million Lilly grant in 2000, the College received a $500,000 extension grant in 2005 to help fund vocation-oriented programs such as the Christian Scholars Program (CSP), faculty summer seminars, domestic and international mission trips, and support for students exploring seminaries. Beginning in 2004 and continuing to the present, CSP conducts student retreat to Hilton Head, SC, during Fall Break with Bruce Main, President of UrbanPromise Ministries, as the speaker. Even after the 2005 separation from the KBC a significant percentage of incoming students applied to the CSP program, often reaching 70 new students in each class. Since they retain at high rates, they constituted the largest scholarship group on campus, often between 250 and 300 undergraduates. In addition to the retreat, CSP organized mission and service trips to Camden, NJ, Garza (Brazil), Gulf Shores, AL, and Copan Ruinas (Honduras). In 2008, Dr. Sheila Klopfer was named director of the program, taking over from Dr. Roger Ward.

Young Scholars in the Baptist Academy (YSBA), initiated with Lilly Grant funds in 2004, provided a selective academic conference for early-career faculty from Baptist colleges and universities across the U.S. and guided senior scholars to develop essays for publication. The YSBA met in Georgetown, Oxford, Honolulu, and Prague. Papers from the seminars were published in two books and three journal issues, thereby raising the College's profile within the academic Baptist community and among other church-related institutions and scholars.

Following Dr. Moody's departure in 2009, Ward became the Director of the Meetinghouse Programs, and in 2010 those activities were consolidated into the Center for Christian Discernment and Academic Leadership (CDAL). For six years the CDAL organized summer seminars for faculty on vocation and scholarship, and annual "Church and Academy" conferences for pastors and church leaders. These conferences featured notable speakers such as Paul Fiddes, Nicholas Wolterstorff, Sarah Ruden, Will Willimon, Stephanie Paulsell, Molly Marshall, Miroslav Volf, Elizabeth Newman, and Wendell Berry.

The Marshall Center for Christian Ministry (MCCM) was directed by Dr. Eric Fruge, who worked closely with the Trustee Board. Several high-profile activities included Christian leadership awards presented to students, faculty, and staff during the baccalaureate service before graduation. The MCCM also funded the gift of a Bible to each graduating student. These awards and gifts provided an iconic continuity with the College's Christian origin and mission. The MCCM funded the George Walker Redding Memorial Lecture. A 1927 graduate, Dr. Redding (1943-1973) was a long-time Bible professor at the College, a

Shakespearean actor, and an active participant in desegregating the College campus and Georgetown Baptist Church in the 1950s. Ken Holden assumed the director role of the MCCM in 2006. Building on a Spring Break trip initiated by former campus minister Sharon Felton, Holden organized ministry trips to Mission Arlington in Arlington, TX. These trips often drew 50 or more students, which some participating for several years. He also expanded the role of the MCCM to include funding for student-initiated mission travel. The MCCM supported pastors with an annual preaching conference on campus in honor of Eugene Enlow ('44), a towering figure in Kentucky Baptist life.

The changing theological and political landscape of Baptist life was evident in the seminaries selected by graduates from Georgetown College. Before the separation from the KBC, often 10 or more students began seminary studies at Southern Seminary. After the separation, that number declined to five or fewer. More students attended Baptist-related seminaries such as Baptist Theological Seminary at Richmond (BTSR), Beeson Divinity School at Samford University, McAfee School of Theology at Mercer University, and George W. Truett Theological Seminary at Baylor University, but they also branched out to include Duke Divinity School, Princeton Theological Seminary, and Yale Divinity School. Female seminary students found welcome especially at Truett and BTSR, and several have returned to pastor churches in Kentucky.

In conclusion, the sea-change of the separation from the Kentucky Baptist Convention altered the orientation of the College's religious activities, although it did not diminish or reduce those activities. Rather, the interest in Christian faith and practice, including vocations of pastoral leadership and theological study, expanded during this time. More students were engaged in mission and service travel, religious retreats, and other extracurricular faith-related activities. The interest and energy related to religious life and racial diversity opportunities enriched the student and faculty experience and buoyed the spirit on campus. At the same time, the sentiment among some faculty members was growing that the change in relationship with the KBC presented an opportunity to redefine the College's approach to Christian higher education. This sentiment increased in light of the process of clarifying the Christian identity statement and the proposed changes to faculty hiring. These actions intertwined in the months leading up to the question of presidential leadership in the fall of 2012.

Chapter 9

Student Life, Greek Life, and Athletics

As a residential College, Georgetown has the benefit of being a living and learning community. The academic focus permeates student housing, social organizations, and athletics. This means there are written and unwritten rules about acceptable behavior and expression of lifestyles. With the separation from the KBC, campus culture began to explore the meaning of this new era. Student Life staff expected an opening of student housing practices and rules that would better align the College with other colleges and universities. The experience of LGBTQ+ students emerged as a focus, especially for student life staff and the faculty. Greek life continued to thrive with high membership, active social programs, intra-organization competitions. The marquis athletic programs of men's basketball and football flourished. For the most part, the campus felt much as it had before the separation, but it was clear that the community was ready for some changes.

Attention to student mental health was an area of noteworthy development. Advances were made in the on-campus counseling center that provided mental health services for students. Megan (Williams) Redditt ('04) developed programs and mentored staff of the counseling center, which was housed in the same building as the health clinic. Under Dr. Todd Gambill's direction, counseling programs were extended into the Greek organizations as well. The tragic suicide of student Remy Okonkwo in November 2007 deeply shocked the College community. The family blamed the Lambda Chi fraternity of foul play, and the news attention cast the College in a negative light. The investigation and subsequent determinations confirmed the death as a suicide. Gambill recalls the event "as the worst day in my professional career." He also noted that through the event and follow-up, the campus united in a shared sense of care and concern for mental health and safety of all its students.

Gambill's responsibilities expanded to include not only student life and religious life, but also athletics, facilities and grounds, auxiliary services, and the Bengals training camp. With this expanded portfolio of management demand, Gambill relied on a cadre of highly effective staff members. James Koeppe developed the Confidence Course at East Campus and trained students to work as facilitators. Groups and organizations outside the College utilized the Challenge Course, which was expanded with a high-ropes extension in 2010. The pre-College retreat Directions continued to attract a high percentage of incoming students, using facilities at the Tim Horton camp near Campbellsville, including water sports and rock-climbing facilities. Faculty and student leaders used the event for cohort development and to address questions and concerns of first-time students with an emphasis on vocation, reflecting the shared funding model of Student Life and the Lilly grant.

With strong enrollments and support from Student life staff, Greek life flourished during this time. Student leadership on campus drew from Greek life and other scholarship and campus groups. Songfest, the musical revue performed during Homecoming weekend, was well supported by alumni and sold out every year. This event was highly competitive among the sororities, especially Sigma Kappa and Kappa Delta. Student life, Greek life, and athletics shared a similar trajectory following the separation from the KBC. The continuing pursuit of industry standards in student life has positioned Georgetown more consistently with similar liberal arts institutions. Greek life offered a profound sense of continuity between current students, their alumni, and the campus culture. Athletic success similarly continued the tradition of excellence that had become synonymous with Georgetown College.

The students were clearly ready for a more robust conversation about housing policies related to expressions of sexuality. The place of gay and lesbian students had been a question from the late 1980s when an alternative student newspaper, *Flipside*, carried stories about exclusion based on sexuality. After the separation from the KBC, students became bolder about their advocacy for gay rights; some displayed pride flags in residence halls, but these were quickly removed. Dr. Jennifer Price, a psychology professor, advocated for LGBTQ+ recognition. A subtle but significant change in the conversation about sexuality came in 2011 with the hiring of Dr. Sarah Cribbs, the College's first openly gay faculty member, to a tenure track position in sociology. Her spouse, Shannon Cribbs, was later hired by Academic Programs. Price was the first faculty sponsor for Campus Spectrum: Gay Straight Alliance, a registered student organization with approval from the administration. Spectrum represented the first College-sanctioned organization advocating for LGBTQ+ issues and visibility on the campus. These efforts coalesced with Dr. Laura Johnson's work as the Title IX coordinator, bringing campus practices into compliance with legal guidelines regarding reports of discrimination, sexual assault, and harassment. In 2012, Price led a faculty effort to write a non-discrimination policy to protect College faculty and staff from being fired for their sexuality. The faculty approved the policy, but the Trustees took no action at that time. (See Chapter 17 for a detailed account of this effort.)

Despite the general tenor of advancement in student life and campus culture, there were growing concerns among staff related to enrollment and financial challenges. Gambill accepted a job with Indiana University in 2013, and he was succeeded as Dean of Student Life by Johnson.

Athletic success continued at the College with football, men's and women's basketball, and volleyball regularly winning conference championships and competing in national tournaments. Athletic Director Eric Ward was succeeded by Brian Evans. As Vice President of Athletics, Evans was the first African American Athletic Director in the Mid-South Conference and the first African American VP of Georgetown College. The discussion about changing the College's athletic association from the NAIA to the NCAA created dissension and led to the abrupt departure of men's basketball coach Happy Osborne in August

2011, who was succeeded by Chris Briggs. Georgetown's success in athletics provided a strong and increasing driver for student enrollment, especially male student athletes.

Football followed its success in the early 2000s with conference championships in 2005, 2006, and 2010 to 2012. The team qualified for the national tournament in those years, reaching the quarterfinals in 2005 and semifinals in 2011. Men's basketball also strung together regular season championships from 2004 to 2011, with MSC tournament titles in 2007, 2008,

VP of Athletics Brian Evans promotes Chris Briggs to head basketball coach in 2011.

2009, and 2011, national tournament quarterfinals in 2005 and 2012, national tournament semifinals in 2008 and 2011, and the national championship in 2013, during head coach Briggs' second year in that role. The women's basketball team achieved regular season championships in 2005 and 2007, MSC tournament championships in 2006 and 2008, and a national tournament quarterfinal appearance in 2005. Susan Johnson retired after 31 years at Georgetown in 2011, and Andrea McCloskey took the team to a semifinal game of the national championship in 2012. Women's volleyball won regular seasons in 2005, 2007, 2008, 2009 and 2012, and consecutive MSC tournament championships from 2005 to 2009. They played in national tournaments in 2005, 2006, 2008 (quarterfinals), and 2009 (semifinals).

Student Life, Greek Life, and Athletics

In 2011, President Crouch initiated a year-long "exploration" of switching the College to the NCAA Division III, a non-scholarship division, similar to moves made by nearby Transylvania University and Centre College. The proposal caused significant friction among the coaching staff, especially those in football and basketball. Due to this possibility and unsatisfactory responses about the College's intentions to become a Division III school, basketball head coach Happy Osborne resigned in August 2011. The Board of Trustees later withdrew from the process without deciding to move out of NAIA. In April 2012, however, the College applied for admission to NCAA Division II, which has athletic scholarships. That application was denied by the committee in July 2012, citing that Georgetown "was not ready to enter the process at this time." In the same press release, President Crouch said they would reapply for membership in 2013, but this did not happen. The College remains a member of the Mid-South Conference of the NAIA.

The early success in admissions in the post-2005 period gave energy and hope for the possibilities of change and expansion. The 2008 national financial crisis and the subsequent decline in Georgetown's enrollment effectively dimmed these hopes. Administrative decisions in relation to student life, athletics conferences, and the overall financial outlook began to weigh heavily on the entire College community. The departures of Happy Osborne and Todd Gambill were precursors of more departures of senior leadership in 2012, including Dan Miller ('82), Darryl Callahan, Martha Layne Collins, and Judy Rogers. The effect of these departures, along with the sense that the College was facing difficult challenges, heightened the campus-wide instability. Many questioned the judgment exhibited by the highest-level College administrators.

Chapter 10

Academic Programs and Faculty Hiring

With the College's newly independent status, its leadership focused on programs and activities that would attract attention and students. In 2006, President Crouch initiated the Equine Scholars program, similar in form to the highly successful Christian Scholars and Oxford Scholars programs. The faculty also embraced the time of change to refresh the general education program which had been in its current form for 40 years. The energy of younger faculty led to the Foundations and Core (F&C) program that included a pre-disciplinary course for all first-time students that focused on academic skills. The process of creating, staffing, and evaluating the F&C program required extensive collaborative effort across the faculty, bringing humanities, arts, science, and professional studies faculty into close working relationships. This exercise in faculty-led development also included discussions about the practice of hiring only Christians for the faculty. A less restrictive policy was recommended by faculty but not acted on by the Trustees.[10] The continuing focus on faculty hiring and the goal of achieving Phi Beta Kappa academic standards fell to Academic Programs and the Provost. These projects became more challenging due to the College's financial state and the fluctuating understanding of how to maintain its Christian identity.

The Equine Scholars Program was initiated in 2004 by Larry Smith, a local leader in the equine industry and friend of Dr. Crouch, It officially launched in April 2006, with a ribbon-cutting and support from John Nicholson, the Executive Director of the Kentucky Horse Park, and State Senator Damon Thayer. Jen Budge was the first full-time director of the program.

In the initial class of 14 students, several were from out of state, including California and Hawaii. An article in *US Equestrian Magazine* described the program's goals to empower students "to pursue an academic degree of their choice while teaching them how their interests in the classroom can connect to a career within the equine industry." The Equine Scholars Program was most successful in the 2010s, with as many as 40 students enrolled at one time. The program focused on field experience; it connected students with the local equine industry through job shadowing, interning, and volunteering, which allowed them "to develop a better understanding in areas of the industry unique to their personal interests and goals while gaining valuable professional connections." Budget challenges and difficulty maintaining a full-time director led to the program's end in 2019.

The Oxford Scholars Program remained a keystone in the partnership between Georgetown College and Regent's Park College, Oxford University. Directed by Dr. Brad Hadaway since 1998, this highly competitive program develops students through tutorial-style classes at Georgetown in preparation for their studies at Oxford. In a manner unusual for visiting student programs, the Oxford Program students are enrolled in Oxford University, take courses with its tutors, and have access to all the research materials of the University. The accommodations permit up to five Georgetown students at Oxford in each of its three terms. As an important curriculum of distinction for high-academic students, the Oxford Program has developed into one of the College's high-profile programs.

The general education curriculum at Georgetown followed a model developed in liberal arts institutions in the 1970s. Its "cafeteria" approach, with students selecting introductory courses from among those offered by academic departments, was supplemented by a required two-course historical sequence in either history, English literature, or philosophy, and a two-course requirement in Bible. At a faculty retreat during the fall semester of 2005, the focus shifted to desired outcomes in student understanding and formation. This conversation spurred a complete revision of the general education program over the next five years. Notable additions would be a Foundations 111 common course for first-semester students followed by a Foundations 112 course in the second-semester that is discipline-specific. Over the years more than 50 faculty members drawn from nearly every major staffed the volunteer curriculum planning committees.[11]

When a voluntary committee of faculty began to explore the idea of developing an academic "core" program in 2007 and 2008, this signaled a different approach to general education. Rather than students selecting content from a menu of academic courses, they would take a progression of courses designed to provide a foundation for their subsequent studies. The benchmark comparisons with institutions similar to Georgetown revealed a remarkable diversity of efforts to accomplish this goal. The General Education Revision Committee formulated a skills-focused course for all students that became the basis for Foundations 111. A subsequent committee in 2008 and 2009 developed the idea of transitioning students from these foundational academic skills into those required in specific departments and majors. Their work formed the basis for the Foundations 112 course.

Drawing upon the research of these committees, the faculty instituted the Foundations and Core program in Fall 2009 and approved the Foundations 111 course the following semester. The program began operation in Fall 2010 under the direction of Dr. Brad Hadaway. The next year the responsibilities for planning and staffing Foundations 111 fell to Dr. Kristin Czarnecki, and Foundations 112 was directed by Dr. Jennifer Price.

A remarkable benefit of this exercise in reshaping the core curriculum was a new sense of community among the faculty. Because Foundations 111 is interdisciplinary, faculty from all departments met for training in the summer before the roll-out of the course. Faculty with expertise in authors or texts led group discussions with the faculty cohort of teachers. Many faculty members engaged in intense and focused academic conversation with faculty with different backgrounds in liberal arts, sciences, fine arts, and professional studies. This collaboration and cohort building strongly unified faculty in their academic mission and mutual support for each others' disciplines and academic abilities.

While researching the various general education curricula at institutions similar to Georgetown, faculty members also became aware of the differing ways that these institutions support their Christian mission through faculty hiring. Also, the Center for Christian Discernment faculty seminars brought leaders of Christian higher education to campus, who introduced the rich tradition of scholarship devoted to the topic of Christian higher education. The conversation about hiring took on a different shape after the separation from Kentucky Baptists since the use of denominational identity was no longer the standard for the College. With the surfacing of interests and expertise of the faculty members during the general education revision process, a broadening sense of the faculty taking responsibility for shaping itself to institutional purpose took root.

This developing sense of faculty responsibility for the ideological shape of the College laid the groundwork for the motion to change the faculty hiring policy described in Chapter 7. The news of the proposal reverberated through the College and the wider community. The hiring policy, more than any other, was understood as the centerpiece of Georgetown's Christian identity. Modifying or eliminating it would fundamentally change the character of the faculty, and hence, the College. When the motion was brought up for a vote in the April 2010 faculty meeting, Dr. Sheila Klopfer offered a substitute motion that referred the policy to the Faculty Committee and instructed it to study the models of hiring at other Christian colleges and universities. A subcommittee of the Faculty Committee was formed to engage in this research and to survey the faculty. Klopfer was selected to chair this subcommittee, but because she was on sabbatical leave during the 2010-2011 academic year, the real work began the following Fall semester. The Trustees, who were informed of the process, asked the subcommittee not to survey students and alumni about the issue of faculty hiring out of fear it would negatively impact the perception of the College. In the process of surveying the faculty, it was found a majority were in favor of opening the hiring process to non-Christians for special curricular needs or institutional purposes. This represented a change from language in the Faculty Handbook

Academic Programs and Faculty Hiring

requirement that states, in several versions, that "all faculty must be Christian," "Christian in fact and in deed," and "willing to support the Christian mission" of the College. Ambiguity arose in defining what is meant by "Christian," and what this entails about a faculty members personal religious practice. It was also unclear what the proposed change to "support the Christian mission of the College" meant. Would this support be simply a statement in writing? What actions, if any, would disqualify a candidate from consideration? One of the stated concerns about the current policy was the awkwardness faculty search committees encountered when it came time to ask a candidate about their Christian commitment and practice, but the proposal did not have a clear resolution for this concern.

Professor of Religion Dr. Sheila Klopfer is instrumental in the review of faculty hiring.

The final report of the subcommittee, with detailed survey information and research on other approaches to hiring Christian faculty, was presented to the faculty in April 2012. The Faculty Committee brought the following motion to the September 2012 faculty meeting, and it came to a vote in October 2012:

> The faculty of Georgetown College propose that the Board of Trustees open the hiring practices of tenure-track faculty at the College to Christians and non-Christians who contribute positively to the

Christian identity of the College and that they empower the faculty to create an implementation committee that will be guided by the Final Findings and Recommendations and the Final Compiled Research of the Subcommittee on Faculty Hiring.

The motion passed by a small margin. This two-year-long process of considering faculty hiring concluded just a few weeks after President Crouch announced his decision to leave his position, also at the behest of a faculty movement (which will be described in Chapter 12). The complicated overlay of questions concerning leadership, Christian character and faculty hiring, and the future of the College in a time of transition combined to make Fall 2012 a very tumultuous semester. The Trustees never acted on the policy proposed by the faculty, and the language regarding Christian hiring in the Faculty Handbook and Contracts remains unchanged.

During this era Georgetown faculty continued to develop new programs of study, often involving travel, to enrich the student experience. For instance, in 2001, Dr. Michael Cairo of the Political Science Department had begun a course titled "Model United Nations." Students participated in the American Model United Nations (AMUN) conference in Chicago, which includes about 1,400 students from colleges and universities across the nation. Dr. Melissa Scheier revived the class in 2008, and takes twelve to fifteen Georgetown students to the conference each year. In 2001, Dr. Rick Kopp, Dr. Mark Christensen, and Dr. Bill Stevens traveled to Belize to scout possible sites for a biology field trip. They applied for funding through the Cooperative Center for Study Abroad (CCSA), and the class attracted sufficient students in 2003. The course, offered in even summers, is sometimes taught by Dr. Tim Griffith and Dr. Tracy Livingston. Kopp estimates more than 50 Georgetown students have participated in this experience. In 2011, Bill Stevens started a May course trip to the western United States to study rocks and fossils. This two-week van excursion is now Georgetown lore: a 5000-mile tour through 14 states to visit the Petrified Forest, Dinosaur National Monument, and Badlands National Park. More than 45 students have participated in this

Academic Programs and Faculty Hiring

adventure. Other new programs utilized the campus as a location for student learning and conferencing. In March 2012, Dr. Regan Lookadoo in the Psychology Department organized a three-day conference on Human Trafficking, the first conference on the topic held in the state of Kentucky. This high-visibility meeting drew speakers and attendees from across the country, with many of the speakers visiting classrooms to provide additional instruction. The keynote address was delivered by Theresa Flores of Gracehaven House. This event is just one instance of Georgetown faculty creating short-term programs to expand the educational footprint beyond the classroom. Such programs challenge and inform students and the community on important issues relevant to the Christian mission of the College.

Chapter 11

Leadership Questions and Finances

In January 2006, the Southern Association of Colleges and Schools (SACS) announced they were removing Georgetown from probation due to non-compliance for financial stability. Jim Moak, the Chief Financial Officer, said in a press release the College's total assets had rebounded from $44.2 million to $52.4 million.[12] President Crouch said the College had had a fine couple of months. Indeed, after the successful vote at the Kentucky Baptist Convention approving the independent status, the College had raised $4.9 million in unrestricted gifts. This was a record for the College and boded well for its new phase of life.

Dan Miller ('87), a fundraiser with WHAS Crusade for Children fund, had taken over as Director of Institutional Development in 2005. Success in the first year of his work lifted the hopes of the College. Plans were in place for a capital campaign to establish the College's financial position for campus development, pursue Phi Beta Kappa standards with faculty development, and bolster the endowment that seemed stuck at the $30 million level. These plans, however, would be challenged by the 2008 national financial crisis that was exacerbated by internal management issues and the loss of senior leadership in 2011 and 2012.

Georgetown had been placed on probation for non-compliance with the standard of financial stability after three years of negative annual budgets ending in 2003. This was the first time the College had received a sanction from SACS related to its accreditation, and it was an early sign that financial difficulties were mounting. Faculty expressed concerns about the financial management of the College and asked Chief Financial

Officer Frank Mason probing questions. Mason was candid in his responses, and this may have contributed to his being fired in 2003. His replacement, Jim Moak, upheld the administration's explanations and presented a confident picture of the College's finances. Nevertheless, Georgetown College was placed on probation in December 2004 for financial concerns and failing to demonstrate compliance with the requirement for maintaining financial stability.

The College was able to address the financial concerns in a year, and its net assets rebounded to $52 million, according to Moak. SACS gave the College a clean bill of health and removed the probation in January 2006. The horizon seemed much rosier for the College. New faculty members were being hired, and the academic program was expanding its vision for developing student excellence. Even with the expected decline of the Kentucky Baptist Convention's $1.2 million contribution over the next four years, the affirmation by SACS of the College's bill of health gave the community confidence for the future.

What the College needed most was a substantial infusion of capital to reshape its future. Although a capital campaign had been suggested in Trustee conversations in 2000, the time had not been right for this major step. But now, with the change in Trustee appointment criteria and the success of the Foundation Board in identifying friends of the College with substantial financial assets, the campaign was begun. Eric Fruge collaborated with a consulting firm in Louisville to determine the target amount and schedule the silent phase of Higher Ground Capital Campaign. Its title, borrowed from a well-known hymn, resonated with the College community.

There was disagreement regarding the financial goal for the campaign, as consultants recommended $44 million but Trustees approved a $72 million goal. The process began and the initial commitments of gifts supported the campaign timeline. However, as the capital campaign was underway, the College's annual budget began to show signs of stress.

Each year the College budgets an Annual Fund of unrestricted income, which is for gifts that can be spent on anything determined by the administration. This is in contrast to

Leadership Questions and Finances

the restricted funds that are given for specific purposes defined by the donors. In the five years prior to the College's separation from the KBC, unrestricted gifts to the Annual Fund had averaged $3.94 million per year, and restricted gifts averaged $3.7 million. The former fell just short of the budgeted $4 million for unrestricted gifts, which included the $1.2 million contribution from the KBC. After 2006 and according to plan, the KBC contribution declined by 25% each year: to $975,000 in 2007, $650,000 in 2008, $325,000 in 2009, and finally zero in 2010. But the College continued to budget the $4 million per year Annual Fund. As the Annual Fund gifts declined to $3.3 million in 2006, $2.1 million in 2007 and 2008, and $1.2 million in 2009, the College entered into a full-blown financial crisis.

The 2008 financial crisis in the nation contributed to the decline in support for the College. The massive drop in the stock market and the sudden insecurity about the future of global finances led to a spike in unemployment in the U.S. and around the world. The impact on interest rates also meant the College's bond agreements were suddenly requiring more money than budgeted to pay the debt service. In the wake of these developments the administration decided to shift the focus of the development staff to the Annual Fund. The capital campaign was abandoned in 2009.

The challenges with fundraising soon led to the departure of Dan Miller, Vice President for Institutional Advancement, who resigned in late 2010. Johnnie Johnson, the Director of Admissions, was reassigned as a senior enrollment counselor in 2010 and then he left the College in 2011. Garvel Kindrick ('85), Vice President for Enrollment, departed in 2012. Martha Layne Collins also resigned her position that year. Collins, a former Lieutenant Governor and then Governor of Kentucky, had joined the administration in 1998 as "executive scholar in residence" to be an ambassador for the College, especially among business and government leaders. She had developed the Global Scholars Program to attract students from other countries, especially Japan, Brazil, and Argentina. This involved significant international travel by College personnel, but was not effective in attracting students. While each of these departures occurred for its own reasons, the cumulative effect was profound on the College community.

Some faculty members looked for opportunities to leave the College as well. They became worried because finding another position was not as easy for them as for staff. In the best of times, faculty moves usually encompass a full calendar year, and in this time period the market conditions made faculty positions rare. The turnover at the senior level of administration was a signal something was seriously wrong at the College, but faculty

Former Governor Martha Layne Collins represents the College among business and government leaders.

members were unable to learn much about the financial condition of the College and whether their jobs were at risk.

Another episode unnerved the community. In late 2011, Dr. Crouch struck up a conversation in an airport with Sergeant Major Fenton Reese (USMC retired), who was the CEO of Veterans in Pursuit of Prosperity (VIPP). Based on this contact, Crouch initiated the development of GC Vets Scholars, a web-based curriculum for veterans to complete degrees at Georgetown. The College invested several hundred thousand dollars in startup costs, hiring Theresa Scates as a full-time developer of the program and purchasing laptop computers for faculty who agreed to create courses in summer 2012. The contract with VIPP for identifying suitable students for

Leadership Questions and Finances 89

enrollment in the program paid $75,000. However, only nine students were identified, and none of them completed the program. The contract was suspended in August 2012. While the venture was unsuccessful, it demonstrated the ability of faculty and administration to create online curriculum and classes.

The administration had been willing to invest significant amounts of money in an unproven program initiated by accidental circumstances. Both its rushed development in the absence of careful institutional consideration and the inconsistency of making risky investments when salaries and benefits for continuing employees were either reduced or unchanged for several years further undermined faculty and staff trust of College leadership.

Faced with declining enrollment and mounting financial struggles at the College, the new Chair of the Trustees, Earl Goode, sought the assistance of the Kaludis Consulting Group from Nashville, TN. Beginning in early 2011, the group conducted interviews with faculty and program directors, and was given full access to the financial information of the College. Their year-long review culminated in a report to the Trustees titled "Finding the Way," which said the path forward for the College would entail financial discipline and deep revisions to its academic program. When the judgment of the consulting group was shared across campus, there was deep disappointment and anger. The Kaludis plan called for the elimination of six majors, including all the languages and music. The Music Department had once been the pride of the College and one of the institutional calling cards connecting it with the churches. Proposing the elimination of this department sounded like a death knell for the College's identity.

The Kaludis plan was adopted by the Trustees, and the reduction of academic programs proceeded over the next year with work by a special faculty committee, the Program Reduction Task Force. Although the plan called for a reduction of twenty-six faculty positions, this was not fully implemented. In the end, only one or two positions were eliminated; other faculty members were lost to attrition and retirement. The impact of this exercise, however, was overshadowed by the suspicion that the College administration and Trustee control had failed the larger College community. This sentiment led to faculty action in September 2012, requesting a change in presidential leadership.

Chapter 12

Faculty Action and Its Result

Fine weather graced the Georgetown commencement exercises in May 2012. Students graduating that year had endured the insecurities of the 2008 financial crisis, but the economy was showing signs of improvement, and they were finding jobs or continuing their education at graduate schools. From the perspective of the families and alumni visiting the campus, the College appeared as it always had: with its stately and beautiful grounds, an admired faculty, and the enthusiastic and happy graduates ready to face the world in a new phase of life. The College also passed its 2012 decennial review with SACSCOC without any issues.

Enrollment projections for Fall 2012, however, were not encouraging. The Vice President for Enrollment, Michelle Lynch, was in her second year at Georgetown. Fall 2011 enrollment had not matched her projections, but she was confident that her staff and plan would improve their performance in the next year. As that year developed, the signs were again pointing to lower enrollment, and faculty members were losing confidence in Lynch's ability to correct the issues. It was a summer of discontent, waiting for the results from the enrollment office and wondering what impact another year of reduced enrollment would mean for the College and their future employment.

Dr. Crouch was aware of the challenges facing the College, especially in the wake of the recent departures of senior administration members. A sense of impending bad news pervaded conversations at social gatherings among faculty over the summer. Sensing these concerns, Crouch organized listening sessions with academic departments in the first week of the new semester. His effort was clear: faculty members were deeply worried about the state of the College, and he was the key person to assuage their concerns and establish a vision for the coming year and a positive direction for the College.

The result of these meetings was not reassuring. Explanations of the decline in enrollment did not address the prevailing worries about the effectiveness of the Vice President for Enrollment. Neither did Dr. Crouch's plan for correcting the College's finances by waiting for future gifts. One faculty member reportedly confronted the President in one of these department conversations and asked, "Why don't you resign?" The pre-semester faculty workshop was overshadowed by the question of whether anything could be done to address the dire situation. Whispers of a vote of no confidence in the President circulated among the faculty. But there was a worry that such a public action would further dim the prospects for the College and its enrollment by creating a harmful public relations moment.

A small group of humanities faculty began to explore options for a faculty action that did not include a public vote of no-confidence for President Crouch. Surreptitiously, this group reached out to other faculty they personally knew were interested in a collective action to bring their concerns to the attention of the Trustees. A plan was developed to write a letter to the full Board of Trustees asking them to consider a change of leadership at the College. If ten tenured faculty members would sign the letter, then other tenured faculty would be invited to add their signatures. If the number of tenured faculty signing the letter reached 20, then it would be sent to the Trustees. As the work progressed, the number reached 27. A later signature brought the total to 28, which was half of the faculty who were canvassed. The letter was mailed to the full Board of Trustees on August 29 and a copy was hand delivered to the president's office. The faculty who signed the letter were aware of the likely repercussions of their action. Crouch had previously insisted that faculty should not contact Trustees directly, but instead share their concerns through his office. Other faculty who had challenged the President soon retired or left the College. The signers were crossing a line they believed could invite retribution or termination of their employment. Once the letter was mailed, the wait for a response began.

The wait, it turned out, was surprisingly short. A copy of the letter delivered to the president's office was faxed to the Board of Trustees Chair, Earl Goode. Goode quickly sent an email to all faculty announcing he and other representatives of the Trustees were aware of the faculty concerns and would meet with "the 27 faculty who signed the letter" as well as the full faculty on September 29. The public announcement of the action by "the 27" was a surprise to many faculty members and the wider College community. Students became aware of the movement and developed a logo that appeared on Facebook and quickly went viral. In a very brief time, the news of the faculty action became widely known, although "the 27" had decided to remain unnamed in the process and not to identify any one spokesperson for the group. By consensus, "the 27" had decided to act only in the collective action of sending a letter. With a scheduled meeting, however, a more detailed account of their concerns and proposals was required. Four members were chosen to represent the group in the meeting with the Trustees: Dr. Sheila Klopfer (Religion), Dr. Karyn McKenzie (Psychology), Dr. Roger Ward (Philosophy), and Dr. Homer White (Mathematics, Physics, and Computer Science). They prepared a script for the meeting and rehearsed it with the group to make sure their representation of faculty concerns was accurate.

The meeting was held in the East Campus Conference Center. Earl Goode, Granetta Blevins, and William 'B. I.' Houston represented the Trustees. Students flanked the sidewalk to the building with signs bearing a student-created logo of "the 27" and cheered the faculty members as they entered. By agreement, no recordings of the meeting were made, but the script of the four presenters was preserved, and notes were taken by the Administrative Assistant to the Provost. The argument was that although Crouch had brought admirable and needed changes to the College, the current financial and enrollment problems could not be repaired by him. Thus, new leadership was requested. In the follow-up question-and-answer period, other long-term and highly respected faculty urged the Trustees to consider a change of leadership. The meeting that followed included all faculty members, and Goode repeated his commitment to the group that the Trustees were aware of their concerns and would deliberate about the best way forward.

An uneasy silence followed the day of the meeting. There was no plan for any follow-up by "the 27," so officially their work was done, and they no longer met as a group. Faculty returned to teaching, and the work of the College continued, albeit in an uncomfortable state of expectation. What if the Trustees ignored

Support the 27

The students create and distribute this logo in support of the faculty members.

their request? Or what if the president acted against those faculty members who had signed the letter? The debate on social media raged with comments for and against President Crouch, and Trustees worried about the damage to the College's reputation that might follow.

Again, the wait was short. On Tuesday, October 2, Crouch informed the College community that he would be stepping down as president at the end of the 2012-2013 academic year. Earl Goode followed this announcement with a plan by the Trustees to organize a celebration of Crouch's long tenure as president of the College.

The success of the faculty action and the decision by the Trustees to select new leadership peaked in emotion and

Faculty Action and Its Result

consequence so quickly that it left the campus in a perplexed state. A momentous thing had occurred, but the College operation and classes, sports practices and games, committee meetings and interactions carried on normally. What the decision would mean for the College and its future began to take shape over the next few months as plans to search for a new president were made and the faculty began their work on implementing the Kaludis proposals for program elimination and faculty reduction. The transition was underway, and what the College would look like on the other side was unknown.

Chapter 13

Legacies of the Crouch Years

Evaluating the 22 years of Bill Crouch's presidency of Georgetown College is a complex assignment. When he became president in 1991, Georgetown was a small, relatively unknown denominational College. His presidency changed its profile to some degree. His efforts to elevate the College to national recognition among top-tier liberal arts colleges only partially succeeded. National championships in football and basketball added to the public profile. The Oxford Program, coupled with programs for theological exploration of vocation, such as the Young Scholars in the Baptist Academy and conferences by the Center for Christian Discernment, increased the College's reputation among Baptist and Christian higher-education circles. The science faculty thrived, sending many students to medical school and securing the College's reputation as a solid preparation for professional programs and graduate school. The Bishop Scholars and Diversity Office initiated an astounding sea-change in the diversity of the student body, tripling the percentage of students of color on campus in just a few years. Further, Crouch had courageously separated Georgetown College from the Kentucky Baptist Convention while advocating for the retention of its Christian and Baptist character. This single action would have the most permanent impact on the future of Georgetown College as an independent, Christian liberal arts institution.

On the other hand, the College had severed its tie to its longest and most secure constituency and lost the goodwill of many Kentucky Baptists. The building construction program of the late 1990s and early 2000s ballooned the institutional debt to

$42 million. Fundraising was successful, raising $76 million in restricted gifts over Crouch's tenure, but this did not translate into the kinds of investments needed to enhance the residential student experience or address the flagging salaries and benefits of faculty and staff. Senior leadership of the College left for other positions for a variety of reasons, but their departures signaled a stalled or unconvincing narrative of change and growth. In addition, the College's Christian mission remained undefined and disconnected from institutional investments and goals.

With his wife Jan, Dr. Bill Crouch serves Georgetown College as President for 22 years.

As the leadership narrative of the Crouch administration waned, the spirit of faculty self-direction and determination expanded. Perhaps this was the organic result of a cohort of highly trained and successful academics who were able to shift their focus from individual research to questions of institutional viability and strength. The impact of faculty leadership on the future of the College replaced what had been most often supplied by pastors and denominational leaders in previous forms of the College's life. Faculty cared deeply about their students and their education, and they also cared deeply for the meaning of the College as a representative of Christian higher education that was faithful to principles of justice and righteousness. The Spirit moved, it seemed, through the faculty to sustain the central characteristic of the College: providing excellent education with fidelity to the best parts of the Christian and Baptist tradition.

Part 3

Bright Hope for Tomorrow

Transitions in leadership, especially after a long presidency like Bill Crouch's, are difficult for any institution. Questions of guiding values and institutional character merge with concerns about operations and finances. Because most of the faculty and staff at the College had been hired during the Crouch administration, this meant facing these questions without a lot of practice of major transition or experience in facing issues of institutional identity and values. Further, given the radical change in Georgetown College's relationship with the Baptist community, how would the Christian mission of the College be adapted to the new landscape? The independence of self-direction gained in the faculty movement did empower the faculty with confidence in their collective judgment and power to affect the direction of the College. This newly realized voice increased the range of options about who would be making the suggestions of how to move forward. Certainly, the Trustees would take a lead, but the heart of any College is the faculty and its academic program. It seemed the College was emerging from a cloistered path bounded by old-growth hedges and turning a corner to find a broad expanse stretching out with only the vaguest hint of pathway ahead and without a clear sight of the next destination point or guide.

The change in status from a denominationally related College to an independent Christian College also altered the skills and experience required in leadership. The search for a president to replace Crouch reflected the uncertainty of Georgetown's mission and goals. The search began in early spring of 2013, but it failed to find the right candidate. Granetta Blevins, alumna and former Chair of Trustees, was named Acting President in June. She served until Dr. M. Dwaine Greene, a long-serving Provost at Campbell University in Buies Creek, NC, began in October 2013. Georgetown was placed on SACSOC sanction in 2014 for financial conditions he inherited. Greene stabilized the College's finances and moved it in a positive direction. His plan for adding masters-level programs was frustrated by the continuation of the sanction for three subsequent years. Although Georgetown was removed from SACSOC sanction in July 2018, Greene decided to leave his position at the end of his contract in October 2018 to allow for a longer-term leader to bring the College to a more stable operation. Greene stayed for eight additional months at the request of the Trustees to ease the transition.

Even the brief period of financial stability under Greene lifted the expectations of the College community from survival to thriving. The selection of Will Jones as president in July 2019 fulfilled this expectation. Jones brought energy and new ideas to the College's operation and jump-started enrollment with Legacy and Legends, a full-tuition scholarship for local high school graduates. That momentum was checked in March, 2020, when COVID-19 caused the College to pivot operations and rapidly shift to online classes. Since the business model depended on revenues from student housing and board, having students return to campus was a priority. With exceptional leadership and work this was accomplished and the Fall semester of 2020 was on campus and in-person. Despite the challenge of the pandemic, enrollment was sustained at around 1,200 undergraduates, a good number and a sign of resilience for the College. Trouble had been brewing, however, at the administrative level. Fractured relationships and questionable behavior by Jones started during the COVID response and developed into a full-blown personnel crisis that came to a head in November 2021. Jones was terminated as President by the Trustees. The College community was shocked.

Dr. Rosemary Allen, Provost, was named Acting President in November and confirmed as President in January 2022. In her first year, the existential threat of the College's financial crisis came into full view when the bank required $2.5 million of principal payment and did not agree to refinance the remaining bond repayment. Facing the onerous terms of principal and interest repayment, coupled with another sanction for financial instability by SACSOC in December 2022, Allen would have to resolve the $28.5 million debt problem if the College was to survive. Beginning in the summer of 2023, she and Trustee Frank Penn ('68) developed and implemented a plan called "Bright Hope for Tomorrow," a phrase from Allen's favorite hymn, "Great is Thy Faithfulness," often sung at baccalaureate services. In nine months, they raised the entire amount from 45 donors, including a $16 million gift from Robert N. Wilson, a 1962 graduate. This was the largest single gift in the College's history. The complete elimination of institutional debt in May 2024 avoided almost certain financial dissolution. It demonstrated the depth of communal resolve to sustain Georgetown College and its mission. The stunning success of this financial salvation, orchestrated by an English professor turned president, no less, signaled a turn from a future-oriented hope that things would improve "someday" to the changes for the good of the College that were possible here and now. A new courage emerged among the College community to face the most difficult challenges and pursue the next right steps.

During the 12-year period from the end of Crouch's presidency to the elimination of the debt, Georgetown College experienced its lowest student enrollment in fifty years. The reduction in tuition revenue strained the College finances. Employees suffered a steep reduction to benefits and no salary growth or cost of living increases to counter inflation rates. Despite these difficult financial conditions, the faculty and staff sustained their high level of attention to academic excellence and responsive student services. Several grants from the Lilly Endowment and NetVUE for vocation programs boosted morale and contributed to a sense of continued growth and development. The Oxford Honors program continued to attract high-performing students and provided research opportunities for faculty in Oxford with accommodations at Regent's Park College. A $1 million grant from Toyota advanced STEM majors at the College, and the American Rescue Plan, which provided COVID-19 relief for employers and institutions, also helped sustain the College through its deep financial crisis. Through all these challenges faculty and staff rallied together to support the institution, exhibiting confidence in the leadership that had developed within its ranks, especially Dr. Allen and Dr. Jonathan Sands Wise. Sands Wise had been named Vice President for Enrollment by Greene, and Jones appointed him to lead the COVID response efforts. The successful response to these two crises positioned him to be named Provost when Dr. Allen became President.

The way forward for Georgetown College has taken shape in a way no one could have anticipated in 2012. With a leadership crisis behind the College and a strong vote of confidence from the supporting community, the way forward is becoming evident. The College community is more aware of the need for a clear articulation of its Christian mission in the changing landscape of higher education. The financial and enrollment challenges that will determine the mid-term and long-term survival of the College stand out in stark relief. There is confidence in the next positive steps and in the current leadership to bring everyone together into the work of overcoming these challenges. And yet, much uncertainty and fear remains about the next phase of the College's life as constituents seek the next horizon of success and thriving. "On we go," as President Greene used to say, as the campus community steps out into this next stage of the life and mission of Georgetown College.

Chapter 14

The Dwaine Greene Presidency

After Bill Crouch announced his departure in October 2012, he remained in his position the remainder of the academic year. The purpose of this period was to properly acknowledge and celebrate his tenure and successes, but it made for a very awkward year. There was animus on the part of those faculty members who considered Crouch fully responsible for the desperately bad financial situation and yet had to work with him and present a positive face for student and faculty recruitment. On the other hand, some faculty and staff resented the disruption caused by "the 27," and some students admired Crouch and valued his personal support for them. In addition to these conflicting emotions and perceptions, a search for his replacement was ongoing in Spring 2013 while he was still in office and on campus.

As the search developed, three candidates were invited to campus to meet faculty and staff and address them during a public meeting in the Chapel. The concerns of the College community were clear: they sought a candidate with deep experience in managing a liberal arts education institution, who had a reasonable plan for addressing the College's debt, and who could provide a compelling vision of the College's Christian and Baptist mission. One candidate withdrew his name shortly after the visit, and the other two did not secure sufficient support to continue the process. The search failed, and the Trustees announced they would restart the process after some time of deliberation and planning.

As an interim solution, Granetta Blevins was named Acting President. Blevins was an alumna who had served in the past as the Chair of Trustees. She had management and financial experience as a consultant with Fortune 500 companies. She had been the Acting Chief Financial Officer at the College during a transition period in that office. Blevins lifted the morale of the College with her managerial confidence and effusive energy when it was most needed in the time of insecurity about the College's direction.

Deep into July, word came that a new candidate for President had emerged. This was a welcome surprise, especially when the candidate's credentials were shared. Dr. M. Dwaine Greene was a long-term Provost at Campbell University, a sister Baptist institution located in Buies Creek, NC. During Greene's tenure, Campbell had developed a broad range of graduate-level programs in Law, Pharmacy, Nursing, and Education, and was thriving. On August 5, the Trustees announced Greene would be the next President, with a start date of October 21, 2013. The delay was necessary for Greene to complete his duties at Campbell and fulfill an obligation to attend commencement exercises at a satellite campus in Kuala Lumpur.

There is an interesting story behind Greene's decision to leave his secure position at Campbell University and take on the challenges facing Georgetown College. Trustee Chair Earl Goode had a friend in the California Community College system who knew Greene from SACS work and recommended him for the job. An early conversation about the Georgetown position was welcomed by Greene, but he dismissed it because he was very content in his role at Campbell. During follow-up calls, the state of the College and its needs became clearer. Greene recounts he had always considered Georgetown an important Baptist College with a rich tradition and an important role in Christian higher education, one that ought to be saved if it could be. In prayer and in conversations with his wife, Carolyn, he became convinced his comfort should not be privileged to the need of such a fine institution as Georgetown. He realized his skills and experience could help the College through its difficulties. Greene recounts this process as a deeply spiritual experience of recognizing the need of the other and being unsettled by a divine call to respond to that need. Reflecting on this process, he says, "The Lord was working on me." He and Carolyn drove to Georgetown unannounced and surveyed the campus and the town. After that trip they decided not to let their comfort keep them from the adventure of following God's calling.

Blevins recalls a meeting with Greene before he took the position, in which she outlined all the troubles the College was facing. As she describes it, "I wanted him to have all the bad news before he started so he didn't take the job on false premises." He accepted anyway. But the evening before his first Trustee meeting he found the expected budget deficit of $2 million for the year was going to be closer to $4 million. To this shocking introduction, Greene responded with a mixture of acceptance and determination: "On we go." During his presidency, these

First Lady Carolyn and President Dwaine Greene join the College community in October 2013.

words became the institution's mantra: things get harder, but we will follow the same path. On we go.

Greene was contacted by the leadership of the Kentucky Baptist Convention before he began his tenure at Georgetown, as there was interest in bringing the College back into the fold of the Convention. A meeting was arranged at the Baptist Building in Louisville with Paul Chitwood, executive secretary of the KBC. Chitwood began laying out the advantages to Georgetown if it would reconnect with the Convention. As Greene recounts the conversation, he responded by outlining his own education and service to Christian higher education: "What you have here is a guy with a Ph.D. in early Christianity, a tenured professor, and a Provost. What you also see here is a guy with a daughter who is an ordained Baptist minister, of whom her mother and I are extremely proud." This indication of Greene's strong support for women in ministry carried significant theological implications for both Greene and Georgetown. The meeting ended, and there was no more mention of Georgetown returning to the KBC.

Greene showed in other ways that he valued authenticity in how the College presented its institutional identity. For example, he addressed the College's dubious claim to an origin in 1789, long promoted by Crouch and proclaimed on the crescent sign at the College entrance, in College literature, and on clothing. Crouch had adopted 1789 as a founding date based on a map he received from an organization early in his presidency that listed Georgetown as among the earliest colleges in America. That map has been lost, but a connection does exist to the property of Elijah Craig's Rittenhouse Academy, a finishing school advertised in a Lexington newspaper in 1789. The academy property later became the site of the College campus, but Rittenhouse was not an institution of higher education. Early in his presidency, Greene was contacted by local historians and faculty who had reservations about the claim to this early origin. He and Todd Rasberry, VP of Institutional Advancement, decided to return the College's publications and signage to the 1829 date of its incorporation by the Kentucky state government. Another visible sign of recalling the College's tradition was using the seal rather than the coat of arms created after the Oxford program was initiated. The College seal was rediscovered by College Archivist Glenn Taul on a diploma from the 1800s, bearing the Latin motto "Respice Finem," which translates to "consider the end" or "reflect on the goal." Greene said that the coat of arms served as a good symbol of the Oxford program, but the seal reflected the broader sense of the College and was more intimately related to its storied past. Hence, the seal became the preferred icon of the College in its programs and other official documents. (See the Appendix for an image and interpretation of the College seal.)

The Dwaine Greene Presidency

Greene inherited an extremely bleak financial position. One of the first issues he addressed was the low student/faculty ratio, which Georgetown could not afford to maintain. A target ratio would be 15:1, but due to enrollment decline the student to faculty ratio approached 11:1. Reaching the target would entail reducing the number of tenured faculty. A faculty-led Program Discontinuance Task Force had made recommendations the previous year to reduce programs, but the end result had been only a minor change. In April 2014 Greene followed the recommendations of the Kaludis report and with the support of the Trustees initiated the elimination of four programs: French, German, Music, and Computer Science, as well as releasing faculty in those areas. The overall reduction of 22 faculty positions was deeply felt across the campus. In addition to long-tenured colleagues losing their jobs, this included several recently hired and highly regarded junior faculty, including Jonathan Sands Wise in Philosophy and J. P. Hanly ('94) in English. Greene and Allen met with each faculty and staff member losing their position, including the president's administrative assistant. The pain was deep, but it was shared across all departments and areas. Some voluntary departures softened the blow. Emily Stowe left her position in languages for a high school teaching job to save other members of her department. Gretchen Lohman in Student Success and James Koeppe in Student Life took positions at a university in Indiana. Sands Wise applied for the Student Success position vacated by Lohman; he moved from faculty into administration in July 2014 and has remained at Georgetown.

Greene postponed his inauguration until the fall semester of 2014 because, in his words, he thought it would be wrong to focus on a celebration when so many people were facing the pain of losing their positions. When it arrived, Greene used his inauguration as an opportunity to introduce a "Strategic Renewal" to refresh the College's operation. The need for a new approach to its organization and finances was made more necessary by the SACSCOC warning in June, 2014. Information from the U.S. Department of Education sent to SACSCOC prompted the accreditor to determine that the College was out of compliance with standards regarding financial stability. Todd

Rasberry described the College's situation in a press release as "a perfect storm" of low enrollment, fallout from the KBC separation, and financial pressure related to the institutional debt. The work ahead was to balance the College's expenditures to income and allow time for faculty and staff reductions to affect the College's finances. This all hinged, to some degree, on addressing the issues of undergraduate student enrollment.

Greene began visiting alumni and supporters of the College, including Chris Coble of the Lilly Endowment. With

Trustees and President Greene recognize Robin Oldham (second from right) for his long service to Georgetown College.

Coble's advice, Greene re-connected the College to the Network for Vocation in Undergraduate Education (NetVUE), a program administered by the Council of Independent Colleges (CIC). This enabled the College to apply for grants dedicated to developing student and faculty programs that enhance the understanding of calling. Greene also made a habit of visiting churches and speaking to community groups. Robin Oldham ('69), who assumed the duties of the executive assistant to the president, aided Greene's work with his deep knowledge of the College's history, supporters, churches, and organizations. Oldham had served in the College administration since the administration of Robert Mills and had personal knowledge of the Eddleman presidency before that. When Oldham concluded

The Dwaine Greene Presidency

his career at Georgetown in 2019, he had served more presidents than any other person in the College's history. Greene and the College benefited from Oldham's profound institutional knowledge and deep personal commitment.

Personnel adjustments became necessary across the campus. After 21 faculty members fell under the force-reduction cuts, it was like a body blow to the academic program. Although the cuts were clearly necessary, the work of maintaining the high quality of the academic program became much more difficult. Faculty members postponed sabbatical leaves, took on additional courses, and assumed other part-time institutional work. The academic program had expanded in terms of course offerings during the robust years of the early 2010s, and a new stability of the academic program began to take shape within the framework of the old. Student Life followed the modernization direction Todd Gambill had set before he left in May of 2013. His assistant, Laura Johnson, was promoted to Dean and Vice President of Student Life. She counted Gambill as her mentor, and under her leadership, Student Life developed its staff and programs consistently and efficiently. Brian Evans became Athletics Director after Gambill's departure, and the success of the marquis sports programs continued. Football added to its string of Mid-South Conference Championships and advanced to the semifinals in the national tournament in 2014, and men's basketball won its second national championship in 2016, further solidifying its reputation as one of the elite programs in the NAIA. Under Evans, the College had made a quickly-rejected application for acceptance to NCAA Division II in 2012, and a revised application in 2014 met a similar fate due to financial constraints. However, even these attempts to change athletic affiliation was an indication of the College's active spirit in seeking to reshape its programs to succeed in the new realities of the day.

In spring 2015, Greene rolled out his vision for a five-year plan titled "A Beacon to Guide," a phrase from the College's alma mater. The strategic plan, adopted by the Trustees, called for continuing austerity, stabilizing enrollment, and adding new graduate programs after the College was removed from

SACSCOC sanction. The first task was reversing the decline in student enrollment. After another low result in new student recruiting in 2015, Greene decided to replace the Vice President for Enrollment, Michelle Lynch. The question was who would be willing to take on this role, and how could the College afford an expensive search to fill the position?

The determination that a new person was needed in Enrollment Management was welcomed across campus. Greene's authenticity and diligence were complemented by his astute

Jonathan Sands Wise, in a series of administrative roles, has success in improving student enrollment and retention.

judgment of character and fit for position. He was able to make difficult decisions to advance the good of the College. When Jonathan Sands Wise lost his tenure track job in philosophy, there was a strong expression of support for his work and value, that retaining his skill and presence was desirable. Greene offered him the position of Director of Academic Success. Perhaps it was not what a budding philosopher would want to do as a profession, but Sands Wise was grateful for the opportunity to remain employed and in Georgetown. As it turned out, Sands Wise reshaped the office. He found a software package for tracking student progress and identifying academically struggling students, and this began to improve student retention, a key factor in stabilizing enrollment. In the fall, Sands Wise was called to a meeting with Greene and Allen. He was convinced it was to inform him they were cutting this position too. As Greene began the conversation, Sands Wise waited for the termination language to appear, but it didn't. Rather, Greene was talking about enrollment, an area Sands Wise had no experience in. When he realized he was being offered the Vice President of Enrollment position, he laughed out loud. Greene assured him that his ability to approach new areas with insight and hard work would be valuable assets to the College. Dr. Allen later recounted that she had suggested Sands Wise for this role due to his outstanding work in Student Success. After considering the offer, Sands Wise accepted the role. The next fall, 2016, the College recorded its largest incoming class in five years, and the following years followed the same pattern. One part of the strategic plan had been addressed.

Greene's disciplined approach to finances restored the College's confidence that the operation of the College could succeed. It felt like a corner had been turned, and the College was on its way to becoming a stable place of education and employment. A $1 million gift from Toyota to support STEM scholarships boosted the College's appeal to students interested in engineering arts. In 2016, however, SACSCOC elevated the College's sanction to Probation with a two-year window to address the areas of noncompliance in financial resources and financial stability. The way forward would be more difficult under probation because new programs could not be added to increase enrollment and revenue. Despite the setback, Greene provided a steadying example and trust that good work would eventually be recognized and affirmed.

The Christian mission of the school took on a new shape under Greene. A Baptist in disposition and church attendance, Greene interpreted the Baptist heritage of Georgetown in a broad sense of fostering inquiry into the meaning of life and welcoming students who espoused other religions or no religious tradition. He initiated agreements with Christian high schools in Lexington and Louisville that would use targeted scholarships to encourage their graduates to attend Georgetown. Student Religious Life under the direction of Bryan Langlands expanded the Chapel program to focus on racial diversity, drawing speakers from the churches connected to the College through Robbi Barber, Director of Diversity and the Bishop Scholars Program. Roger Ward, Director for the Center for Christian Discernment and Academic Leadership (CDAL), led several grant projects, including a $600,000 grant from Lilly in 2014 to create Faithways, a summer program for high school youth with Andrew Noe ('08) as its first director. A $300,000 extension grant in 2019 continued this program, with Hollis Dudgeon ('16) serving as program director. In 2016 the College received several grants from NetVUE for staff development and "Vocation across the Academy." This program enriched the students' experience with reflection on calling and meaning, including a common book for the whole campus, *Just Mercy* by Bryan Stevenson. A travel experience to the Legacy Museum and other sites created by the Equal Justice Initiative in Montgomery, AL, was initiated in 2018 as a result of this grant. The Center for Christian Discernment continued its program of January conferences from 2014 to 2018 with speakers including Walter Brueggemann, Sarah Ruden, Will Willimon, Stephanie Paulsell, Miroslav Volf, Wendell Berry, Philip Jenkins, and Norman Wirzba.

The enrollment increase and other positive news from the College were well received in the town of Georgetown. In April 2017, Greene was honored by the Georgetown and Scott County Chamber of Commerce as Citizen of the Year. Clearly abashed at the honor, Greene said, "I have the great blessing to work for something that has such worthy purposes." With careful management of the College's expenses and improvement in enrollment, Greene was able to balance the College's operational budget. With all the markers identified in the probation moving in the right direction, there was hope SACSCOC would lift its sanction so the College could begin to add new programs. But in December 2017 the agency decided to extend the College on probation for another 12 months so the College could prove more adequately its stabilized position. This was devastating news to both Greene and the College.

In reaction to the disheartening news of continued probation, a group of alumni, including Martha Chatham Pryor

The Dwaine Greene Presidency

('79), Laura Owsley ('92), Charlotte (Stickle) Elder ('96), Scott Fitzpatrick ('87), Marsha (Oakes) Eden ('87), and others, created a Facebook page called "Support Georgetown—Love & Loyalty." Their effort had a viral impact, and alumni support for the College surged to more than 25%, shattering previous levels of giving. The Development Office built on this revived support of alumni and the community, and their efforts took on a new vibrancy and concern.

With continued effort and two more strong entering classes, the College's future began to brighten. In June 2018, SACSCOC finally lifted the College's probation. There was a celebration on Giddings Lawn to mark the emergence from this long period of trial. Greene's plan for "strategic renewal" had worked to bring financial stability to the College and paved the way for new programs that would eventually attract new students and generate revenue. However, at the opening session for the faculty in fall of 2018, Dr. Greene announced his plan to leave his position at the end of his five-year contract in October. In his comments to a stunned faculty, Greene acknowledged the College had made remarkable progress and would continue its development. He felt that further progress would depend on a person who could commit to initiating new programs for an additional five years, and he was unable to make that commitment. In his humble way, Greene pointed to the future success of the College as more important than his continuing his role as president. He extended his time at the College beyond his contract date to the end of the academic year to provide a segue to the next president. To honor Greene, the faculty collected funds and commissioned art professor Daniel Graham to build a tool chest from wood of campus trees. It was inscribed with Greene's favorite Bible verse, Micah 6:8, "Act justly, do mercy, and walk humbly with your God." A lacquered box was made for Carolyn Greene with verses from her favorite hymn, "It is well with my soul." These gifts were presented at the last faculty meeting of spring 2019.

Dwaine and Carolyn Greene were deeply admired by faculty, staff, and students. Their presence at sporting events and Carolyn's cookies for students were loved by all, and their spirit of care and confidence permeated the College. In his five and a half years of leadership, Greene provided the College with an example of the positive effects of financial and managerial discipline. Decisions reflected the direction the College needed to move: trimming costs while providing an excellent liberal arts education and maintaining a positive campus environment. Another significant legacy was the realization that the leadership the College needed was already present within its ranks. Identifying and developing the talent already at the College ensured both continuity of institutional knowledge and a focus on the mission-centered character of the faculty and staff. The work of these dedicated individuals reflected the enduring character of the College and their commitment to its Christian mission. Finally, the response of alumni in the "Love and Loyalty" campaign demonstrated that the College had deep and emotional support among its alumni and friends. Such an obvious outpouring of support had not been seen in many years, and it was heartening to hear stories of affirmation and appreciation from so many voices. This support was evoked by Dr. Greene's careful and humble service and would, in a few years, lead to an even more dramatic expression of support.

Chapter 15

The Will Jones Presidency

The farewells to the Greenes were sad in May of 2019, but the communal sense of well-being was evident. The men's basketball team was fresh off a third National Championship in March, and graduation exercises went well despite a relatively small graduating class. The hopes and expectations for a period of good news and progress on the College's horizon were matched by the pleasant weather and the beauty of the campus. The presidential search committee expressed confidence that the person they had identified would continue the path of stability and growth. In fact, there was a hint of glee in their voices. This was not just a candidate, but a good candidate, perhaps even an exciting one.

Their excitement was explained with the appointment of Will Jones in July 2019. Jones was recruited from the presidency of Bethany College in Kansas, a Lutheran institution, but he was a native of Kentucky, a Baptist, with two adopted and four biological children. A graduate of Berea College, Jones came from very humble beginnings to achieve distinction in higher education. The fit with Georgetown's Baptist heritage and its aspirations of succeeding against straightened circumstances was evident and inspiring. Things were looking up for the College, but enrollment was lagging. The number of undergraduate students on campus was hovering in the low 900s. They had increased to 975 in 2016, but the SACSCOC probation the next year helped diminish the number of first-time students by about 50. In Fall 2019, Jones inherited a campus of 930 undergraduate students with 309 new students. Any implementation of the new programs Greene had envisioned and prepared for would be possible only if the College's undergraduate enrollment increased. Jones developed a plan to jump-start enrollment by attracting a larger share of Scott County graduates by providing full-tuition scholarships. This program, "Legacy and Legends," or L&L as it became in shorthand, was extended to four counties with historic ties to the College: Scott, Franklin, Owen, and Casey. The premise of the program was to attract new students to Georgetown who had not considered a private liberal arts institution as an affordable possibility, but above all to get more students on campus as quickly as possible. The extension of L&L to Casey County also reflected the long-time support of a high school from that county and a household income profile that excluded most students from pursuing higher education.

Jones's interest in extending liberal arts education to students and families who may not have considered it an economic option connected with his own biography. His family in Whitley County, KY, did not have the benefit of education. Neither of his parents finished high school and could only find occasional work in low-paying jobs. His parents regularly told Jones that he was going to college. They pushed him to excel in school as the way to expand his opportunities. Fortunately, he fit the profile for Berea College and was accepted. One of the stories Jones shared at Convocation in fall of 2019 was about a yard sale his parents organized to gather funds to buy him a suit for college. Friends and neighbors donated items, including canned goods and various homemade items. With the $200 raised, he was able to buy a suit and a tie, the tie that he was wearing as he gave the speech. This story of rising from impoverished conditions with the support of a community and the liberating effects of a college education resonated deeply with the students and faculty. He concluded his speech with this litany of welcome:

> However much money you have or don't have, you are welcome here. Wherever you are from, nation, state, city, you are welcome here. Whatever religion you hold or don't hold, you are welcome here. However you identify and whoever you love, you are welcome here.

The Will Jones Presidency

This was the first public expression at the College of a message that welcomed and affirmed students who identified as LGBTQ. The Trustees had amended the non-discrimination policy to include sexual identity and expression in 2018, but the strong note of welcome and affirmation changed the tenor of the campus. Jones affirmed this welcome as the principle of Jesus' Sermon on the Mount and the servant leadership presented in the parable of the Good Samaritan. Acts of service and inclusion, Jones said, are the gospel core of a Christian College more than holding dogmatically to doctrine or theology. The powerful example of Jones's history and the attitude of welcome produced a sense of optimism and mission as his tenure began. L&L was approved by the Trustees and announced in December 2019, in time to play a role in recruiting the class of fall 2020. And then COVID-19 came along.

Dr. Doug Figg ('85), director of a lab at the National Institutes of Health, presented a Hatfield Lecture on the relation of science and religion in February 2020. In a conversation afterward, he and Dr. Horace Hambrick, a local pediatrician and Trustee, compared notes on the report of the respiratory infection of a research doctor in China. Figg asked Hambrick, "Have you seen the x-rays of his lungs? They are incredible." Despite the virulence of the pathogen, Figg didn't think it would be a significant challenge to human health and encouraged Hambrick to keep his travel plans to the Holy Land. So surprising was the emergence of the COVID-19 virus worldwide, it even took experts by surprise. Fortunately, the Hambricks canceled their trip as news of the virus and its spread around the world began to fill the news feeds.

As the semester progressed toward Spring Break, concerns about COVID-19 increased, but there were no immediate facts to worry about. Students and faculty departed for trips and conferences. That was the last normal week of class. The first report of COVID infection in Kentucky was in nearby Cynthiana (Harrison County), which was unnervingly also the place where the Walking Dead stories originated. When the NCAA canceled March Madness, it was a signal that the virus was a serious concern, and adjustments were going to begin on a large scale.

Without a clear understanding of how the virus spread or its potential effects on public health, everyone was left in a state of fear. The College extended Spring Break for a week, and then canceled all in-person classes for the remainder of the semester. Based on the experience gained from both the short-lived GC Vets online learning program and the long-standing online Master's program in Education, Academic Programs supported faculty in using Canvas, the College's Learning Management System, to finish classes remotely. Commencement exercises were canceled and graduates were mailed diplomas.

Georgetown College, like the rest of the world, was in a quandary about how to proceed. Would students enroll in college without in-person classes and residence, and how could Georgetown bring them back safely? The College's budget was dependent on tuition and housing fees; without them, it was unclear if the College could survive at all. Jones appointed Sands Wise to manage the COVID adjustments and health protocols for the College. Sands Wise worked with science faculty to use the recommendations of the CDC for infection testing and ventilation. Rosemary Allen, Registrar Jason Snider ('10), and Sands Wise reshaped the entire academic schedule, using new spaces for classrooms and changing housing arrangements to mitigate exposure to the airborne virus. An early test of the modified approach to campus activities was the Christian Scholar Directions Retreat held in July 2020. The sessions and meals were held in a tent erected between Pawling Hall and the Chapel. With 85 new and returning students, the retreat was successful as an early trial for testing and masking protocols for the fall semester.

The modified course schedule divided the semester into sub-sessions of seven weeks with classes meeting for 75 minutes four times a week, on Monday, Tuesday, Thursday, and Friday. To address the problem of speaking while wearing COVID masks in rooms with loud air purifiers, the faculty were issued portable amplifiers. Athletics continued, with modified testing and illness tracking protocols in place. Dr. Rebecca Singer, with the assistance of Alexandria (Smiley) Lopez ('07) in Student Success and Tiera Mason in Student Life, was employed as the testing and quarantine manager, tracing outbreaks of the virus and enforcing on-campus or home quarantine. With their program in place, the number of infections fell to a manageable level, and the semester proceeded surprisingly normally. The Spring semester of 2021 followed the same pattern of sub-sessions and modified mass meeting events. Commencement was held on Giddings Lawn.

Despite the disruption caused by the COVID pandemic, the College functioned surprisingly well. Student conferences and business shifted online; faculty meetings were held via Zoom and were productive, even cheerful. The College initiated a men's volleyball team with the transfer of several Polish players and a coach from a college in Ohio. The cheer squad won a national championship. International travel remained restricted, so the Oxford program also shifted to a remote format. In a letter for GC Magazine in Spring 2021, Jones noted the effect of COVID on the College but also highlighted the College's third-year ranking by the U. S. Department of Education as the best college in Kentucky for job placement of graduates. The Institutional Development office also heralded the success of Giving Day 2021. A record number of 1,111 individual gifts raised $200,000, increasing the percentage of alumni giving by over 20%. This good news continued with Jones' successful renegotiation of the College's bonded debt terms with Fifth Third Bank. As a part of those terms, the bank forgave $3 million in a revolving debt account. The downside was the bank took that short-term line of credit away from the College.

The American Rescue Act of 2020 probably saved the College. Employment in the United States rebounded from the sharp drop caused by the pandemic, and the government support for employers kept money flowing to families. The College also received support from the Paycheck Protection Plan (PPP) for employees and for upgrading air filtering for classrooms. A record entering class of 481 students in fall of 2021 lifted the campus census to 1,225 students.

Homecoming activities in 2021 included a faculty gathering under a tent near the football stadium. This allowed alumni to greet a large group of former professors and introduce their families. The fall day did not disappoint with clear skies on a warm afternoon. Jones had invited Bill and Jan Crouch to return to campus for Homecoming and be recognized at halftime of the football game. This was the first official return of the Crouches since their departure in 2013. Word of their presence had been shared informally among faculty, and the reception was clearly mixed. The drama of this moment, however, was a precursor to a much larger one that had been set in motion two weeks prior.

In mid-October, Jones traveled to Indianapolis with a College employee to attend an event honoring alumnus and former Trustee and Chair, Earl Goode. This employee subsequently filed a police report of a sexual assault as well as a Human Resources complaint at Georgetown College. A Lexington judge granted the employee an Emergency Protective Order that barred Jones from entering Giddings Hall, where the employee also worked.

The Trustees were informed of the situation and quickly investigated the events. On November 2, 2021, the Board of Trustees announced the termination of Jones's tenure as President. This announcement shocked the faculty and the wider College community. As the news settled in, faculty, staff, and students continued their work and classes with a new concern about the state of the College. How would this news affect the College's Christian reputation and its appeal to families as a safe environment for students? What would be the effect on the financial support for the College? How could the College endure this new challenge, as well as the aftereffects of COVID and its ongoing financial and enrollment crisis?

Dr. Rosemary Allen assumed the role of Acting President and began to communicate with the College community the information she could share about this rapid and surprising transition. She named Jonathan Sands Wise as Acting Provost and assured the College that they would work together to support the smooth functioning of the College in the time of transition it had abruptly entered. At the Hanging of the Green event in early December, Allen and her husband Todd Coke read the liturgy for the Christ candle. When she approached the podium, the students and faculty leapt to their feet and gave her a loud and sustained standing ovation. It was the first time anyone could recall the students giving such an ovation for a president, and it was a clear sign that the community was ready for a different kind of leadership.

Will Jones left a deep mark on the College. High hopes and expectations for transforming the College into a more thriving institution came crashing down with a notice of termination. He had two daughters enrolled in the College, and they were well supported by their friends and groups during this experience. The Trustees extended their scholarships so they could continue attending the College, and both have graduated. One mark of the quality of the College community is its concern for protecting and supporting each other in times of need.

Another effect on the College following this incident, however, was a shift in the idea of presidential leadership. Throughout its history, presidents of the College were male, Baptist, and carried themselves like pastors of a church and generally affected a model of authority. Jones was a bit of a departure from this model, although he had a charisma reminiscent of Crouch in presenting a novel and aggressive approach to resolving the College's problems. Still, the College had wanted a strong leader with a new, innovative idea that would align with the College's expectations. The experience with Jones changed that expectation. What the College needed now was a person with competence and character. Flashy speeches had not brought the needed development for the College. We needed a leader who could sort through our problems, access the leadership already present on campus, and rally support from the larger College community.

A further legacy of Jones, perhaps an unfortunate but needed lesson, was the fragility of Georgetown College. Since the time of the College's thriving years in relation to the Kentucky Baptist Convention, and even during the Crouch administration after the separation from the KBC, Georgetown had always carried a sense of solidity and sturdiness. It was an historic and sound institution, a nearly 200-year-old pillar of the community. Faculty, staff, and students could rely on Georgetown in the present and for the future, grounded in the College's historic Christian mission. That security was broken by the escalating challenges of the previous years: first by the financial condition that seemed like a permanent state of the College, then by COVID, and finally by the abrupt collapse of the Jones presidency. The Trustees responded as best they could to this fragility with their quick action and choice of an acting president. But the question of the future of Georgetown College, whether it could in fact survive, came into the thoughts of all who were familiar with its challenges. Responding to this sense of fragility was a new challenge, a new sense of risk that had suddenly appeared in its way.

Chapter 16

A Woman for All Seasons: President Rosemary Allen

In 1984, Dr. Steve May, an English Professor at Georgetown College, was awarded a National Endowment for the Humanities grant for a one-year research leave to Oxford University. The English Department had been unable to find a suitable replacement to teach his classes. It was summer and time was short. May called his former office mate from the University of Chicago, Scott Colley, who taught at Vanderbilt University, and asked if he had a graduate student he could recommend for Georgetown. Colley mentioned the job to a fourth-year graduate student as she walked down the hall outside his office. Rosemary Allen had finished coursework and was writing her dissertation, and some money and teaching experience sounded like a good option. She mailed her credentials and spoke by phone with May, and later drove to Georgetown to interview with President Morgan Patterson. Her adjunct teaching at Belmont, a sister Baptist institution, counted in her favor. She preferred the Belmont students to those at Vanderbilt. Allen took the job and taught full-time. The one-year position expanded, however. Over the next four years, Allen replaced Dr. Gwen Curry ('54) for a year, another year for May's sabbatical, and then taught part-time while she finished her dissertation in 1987. Back in Nashville in the fall of 1988, she was filling a temporary position at Vanderbilt and still looking for a permanent position after turning down a tenure-track job at Gonzaga University. The male-dominated Gonzaga department didn't feel right, and she preferred the teaching setting of a smaller college, like Georgetown. When Dr. Frank Ellers ('54) retired from the English Department due to health reasons, Curry called Allen to fill his position mid-year.

Allen's choice to take a tenure-track position at Georgetown disappointed her Vanderbilt professors, but she liked the liberal arts focus and the character of the department and the students. In 1989, Allen began teaching journalism, a new course for her, staying about a week ahead of her students. Although she arrived on campus to fill the needs of Georgetown College on a temporary basis, the need lasted. In January 2022, she was named Georgetown College's 26th President.

Throughout her long career with Georgetown, Allen has seen the College operation from every possible level of engagement. Her perspective on the pivot points of the College's story show things from an interesting angle, but this perspective is rooted in her primary identification as a teacher and English professor. Allen early distinguished herself as an excellent classroom teacher. She became the Chair of the English Department in 1991 and was awarded the Cawthorne Excellence in Teaching Award in 2002. When Provost William Pollard announced he was taking a position at Transylvania University, Bill Crouch appointed Allen as one-year Acting Provost in 2004. He removed the Acting in 2005, making her the first woman chief academic officer at the College. She was drawn to Crouch's energy and his support of the Phi Beta Kappa initiative, which focused attention on the College's academic quality. Allen had the responsibility of hiring to meet this goal and brought several large classes of new professors to the College.

As part of the leadership team of the College, Allen recalls their shock and surprise when SACSCOC placed Georgetown on probation in December 2004. The SACSCOC Vice President had to tell Bill Crouch twice before it registered. The team from the College—Jim Moak, Garvel Kindrick, and Allen—quickly began making plans to inform the Trustees and disseminate the news to the broader community. That year also included the work and communication leading up to the separation from the KBC. Allen had reports of individuals checking the college bookstore for questionable material and collecting information about the content of classes. She supported the break from the KBC to protect academic independence and open the campus to more progressive attitudes and policies.

Crouch's vision for the campus and building was also attractive to Allen for its embrace of needed upgrades like the Ensor Learning Resource Center. Other building choices seemed to go in odd directions, more for aesthetics than usefulness. The decision to build the East Campus stadium and complex for the Bengals was a good plan with the partnership with the city, but Crouch decided to continue with the plan independently after that agreement fell through. Allen considers that decision as a turning point for the financial health of the College.

The impact of the building program and the decline of support from the KBC mounted into financial pressure on academic programs. Pay raises were deferred in favor of adding new faculty lines, which led to the 2009 funding crisis for raises

Dr. Rosemary Allen has served Georgetown College as faculty member and Provost, and now is its 26th President.

of promoted faculty. There were no years with a surplus, which meant the budget and spending were only going to get tighter. When key leaders began departing in 2011 and 2012, Crouch seemed unable to respond. There was no strategic plan for the College, and the loss of key personnel added to the sense Crouch was grasping at straws.

When the news came that the faculty group had written a letter to the Trustees in September 2012, Allen was grateful that they had avoided the public spectacle of a no-confidence vote.

Allen's former colleagues kept her out of the loop on their action so the focus landed squarely on the president. She sensed Crouch's fear at this development when he asked her if she thought it was serious. He was still searching for the transformational gift that would resolve the College's financial problems. But the time for that had passed. While the Trustees publicly presented a united front for Crouch, she knew there were questions and divisions among the Trustees regarding support for him. The result of the Trustees bringing the Crouch era to an end did not surprise her. She was thankful, however, Crouch was given the chance to gracefully retire and end with a celebration of the positive changes he had brought to the College. Simultaneously, she was becoming more aware of the College's increasingly fragile financial position.

With the end of the Crouch administration, Allen ensured the academic program continued to function smoothly during the transition. Allen worked well with Acting President Granetta Blevins during the interim period, gaining the confidence of the faculty and Trustees as the steady hand in times of transition. When Allen first met Greene off-site, he struck her as measured and serious, but not distant like Patterson. Rather, he asked about the composition of the faculty and the reception he could expect. She thought Greene's approach to management and leadership would be beneficial to the College, given his clear difference style to Bill Crouch. That observation turned out to be quite accurate.

Greene inherited not only the large institutional debt from the previous administration, but also a swollen accounts payable balance. The spending in Crouch's last year left a hole in the operating budget that would have to be filled first by reducing expenses. Allen was aware that Greene had taken the results of the Kaludis report and the findings of the Program Restructuring Task Force, and then conducted his own analysis. Working closely with CFO Jim Moak, Greene developed a plan to reshape the faculty numbers, consistent with maintaining academic quality while balancing the budget. When he told Allen 22 faculty positions had to be eliminated, she was shocked. She had hired many of the people she was now going to have to dismiss, and it hurt. Throughout the process of determining which faculty stayed or left, Allen said Greene never told her what to do, just what had to be achieved.

While the College was planning to reduce academic positions, SACSCOC placed the College on warning in June 2014. This was primarily due to the large accounts payable balance held over from the previous administration, another inheritance Greene and Allen had to address. Throughout the Spring semester, meetings were held with faculty and staff members who were leaving. Some of them self-selected to leave, which eased a bit of the pressure. After Greene's inauguration, the College's finances began to move back toward balance. Allen was surprised it didn't move more quickly in a positive direction and that fundraising was struggling to fill the gap. Todd Rasberry, Greene's choice for VP of Institutional Advancement, was not getting the results either had hoped for. Enrollment also was not making the progress needed, and Greene felt he couldn't trust the numbers presented by VP for Enrollment, Michelle Lynch. Greene decided to replace her with a candidate inside the College, and Allen suggested Jonathan Sands Wise. Allen had seen his initiative and potential with the GC Veterans program and work in Academic Support. It was a risk, but Greene was willing to take thoughtful risks. After that transition and the hiring of John Davis as VP of Advancement, Greene finally had a team all moving in the same direction.

Still, the SACSCOC warning and required reporting hung over the College, preventing it from developing the new programs essential to Greene's strategic renewal plan. According to Allen, Greene wrote all the monitoring reports himself. He wanted SACSCOC to have the case for the College in his own voice. At the same time, Greene was making heroic efforts to keep the College functioning. At one time he had to ask a foundation to change the classification of their funds with the College so they could be used to make payroll. This was a desperate move, successful at the moment, but costly for the College's reputation. Greene was fully aware of the cost and made the difficult choice to sustain the College's employees. When SACSCOC elevated the sanction to Probation in December 2017, despite all the metrics moving in the right direction and the College very close to having a positive number in its unrestricted assets, the blow was too great on Greene. He realized the path to financial stability was longer than he anticipated, longer than he could commit to, and the College needed more support from alumni and donors than he had been able to raise. He had the respect and admiration of many alumni and donors, but it had not turned into the financial support needed for the College to emerge from the downward financial cycle. Greene didn't want to leave the College stranded, and SACSCOC's removal of the College from sanctions in July 2018 helped. But he was tired and had done all he could to move the College forward. Allen respected his selfless devotion to the good of the College and his determination about what was best for its long-term interests. That included leaving his position in 2019 and returning to his family farm in North Carolina.

Will Jones struck Allen as a grass-roots kind of guy, strong-minded and energetic with some of Crouch's charisma. His energy and novel plan to boost enrollment lifted the horizon of the College to the prospect of moving into a more stable position. The early signs of challenge to come appeared with Jones's discomfort around faculty, particularly Allen whom he never called by her first name. It was always "Dr. Allen." During the COVID-19 pandemic, Jones made the right decisions about returning students to campus in Fall 2020 and securing funds from government programs to keep the College afloat. Allen and her team supplied the nuts and bolts of reshaping classrooms and schedules, and everything worked well until it didn't.

Allen had informed faculty earlier that year that her intention was to complete the 2022 decennial review for SACSCOC and then retire. Jones was already making plans for her departure when his own position came to an end. Allen recalls the precise moment she got the call from Trustee Board Chair Robert "Bob" L. Mills ('67). She and her husband Todd had just turned their porch light out after Halloween trick-or-treating ended and sat down to relax. Mills called, and after some small talk, said that he had some unexpected news. Jones was fired. Would she consider stepping in during the interim as Acting President while they got things figured out? She immediately agreed, especially because the SACSCOC report was going to be under review in the next few weeks.

The shock of Jones's termination spread across campus and into the network of the College. Who would lead the College now with the continuing complications of COVID restrictions, a SACSCOC review that was not expected to be good news for the College, a mountain of debt, and the mark of a senior leadership meltdown? As the College had learned with Greene, competence and hard work were necessary for success, but represented only part of the solution. The confidence and support of the larger community were essential for the short-term and long-term life of the College. Meanwhile, the fall semester carried on as normally as possible: holiday celebrations, finals, grades, and students leaving campus for the break. News broke that several lawsuits had been filed against the College for actions related to Jones's termination, increasing the anxiety of College personnel. One hopeful thing was the strong and supportive response to Acting President Rosemary Allen.

On January 3, 2022, the Trustees announced they had chosen Dr. Rosemary Allen as the College's 26th president. Mills recounted a process of confidential, mostly in-person conversations with one College cabinet member, friends in higher education administrative roles in Kentucky, Illinois, and Florida, former President Greene, and six key members of the Board's executive committee. These discussions culminated in the December 14 Executive Committee meeting and the December 15 Board of Trustees meeting. In those meetings, after presenting the strengths, considerations, and caveats of a Dr. Allen presidency, Mills reminded the Board that the usual national search and onboarding process for a permanent president would take up to 18 months. The critical state of the College's finances, an apprehensive cabinet, faculty, staff, and student body, and the SACSCOC relationship all raised the need for a quicker solution. The Board agreed and voted to support this bold move. In a press release, Mills said,

> Dr. Rosemary Allen was the clear choice as Georgetown's next president. Through her longstanding commitment to Georgetown—first

as a faculty member and later as Provost—she has demonstrated with distinction the outstanding qualities we desire in a president to lead this school.

The announcement was met with widespread celebration across the community. Allen was the first woman in the role of president, qualified by her 38-year history with the College and her long record of diligent work and success. Allen announced she was appointing Jonathan Sands Wise as Provost and Executive Vice President. Neither Allen nor Sands Wise had experience in their respective roles, but that appeared secondary to their commitment to the College, individual competencies, and resourcefulness. The full measure of that resourcefulness would be needed to address the College's continuing challenges, especially as SACSCOC placed the College on warning in December 2022 for failing to meet the core requirement of financial stability. This had been expected, and the work of responding was cut out for Allen and Sands Wise.

Aiding this work was a new CFO, Rush Sherman. He had extensive experience with Spalding University in Louisville and had turned their finances around over a decade. Bethany Hornback Langdon ('93) was hired as VP for Communications and Marketing and became VP for Advancement and Communications after the departure of John Davis. Allen presided over her first commencement as president in May, and the College began to relax its COVID policies for the following academic year 2023-2024. As Allen, with Sherman's help, became more familiar with the College's financial situation, it became clear that a lack of timely and accurate financial information was part of the College's problem. With the previous accounting system, there was no way the administration could know its cash position during the year. The true condition was known only when the audit was completed in August. Sherman re-worked both the budgeting process and the accounting system to improve the accuracy and timeliness of the data. While it was beneficial to gain a better understanding of the College's financial situation, that was the end of the good news. The operating budget was still out of balance; the College was spending more than tuition and annual fund contributions could support. Things worsened in 2023, when the bank added a new set of demands for repayment of the bonded debt.

An amended bond agreement with Fifth Third Bank put additional pressure on Georgetown as it approached the 2029 deadline for debt repayment. The College made a $2.5 million principal-only payment in November 2022, but this significantly depleted its cash reserves. The bank created a new schedule for the repayment of principal beginning with $1 million in November 2023 and increasing by $250,000 each year, but it did not renegotiate the debt itself. This meant Georgetown still faced a balloon payment of $18.225 million due in 2029. Allen had no choice but to accept the terms of the amended agreement, but she knew there was no way the College could bring its operating budget to a point where it could support those repayments. In addition, the bank had ended the revolving line of credit in 2019. Georgetown College had no access to short-term borrowing from Fifth Third Bank or any other bank because Fifth Third held liens against all the College's property. It sounded like a death knell for the College.

What the College needed most clearly was to be free of its bonded debt. That was the key to the SACSCOC determination of Georgetown's failure to sustain adequate financial resources in its initial evaluation in 2022. It was preventing any investment in new programs or refurbishment of student housing, which was becoming a serious problem for student recruiting and retention. Allen considered her options. Why would anyone who cared about the College give toward removing this burden of debt? To pay a little bit would be sending dollars down a black hole. Any impact would disappear if the long-term problem wasn't first resolved. But what if a donor could know their gift would be required only if all the debt was paid at once? Would that generate the support needed? Allen thought that kind of approach just might work.

Allen first took her plan to Trustee Frank Penn ('68), who had already been discussing approaches to debt elimination with other Trustees. He liked it, and both he and Allen committed $1 million of their own money as the initial pledges. They arranged the plan so the commitments would only mature with the total amount necessary to remove all the bonded debt. A goal of $20 million was set, with the expectation of negotiating with the bank for handling the $8.5 million balance through debt forgiveness. They, in coordination with Langdon, started contacting donors and quickly brought the total committed to $10 million. One of the final calls was to Robert Wilson, a 1962 alumnus who had had a successful career at Johnson and Johnson and then as a private equity investor. His initial pledge of $5 million was expanded to $7.5 million, with the additional $2.5 million to act as a challenge grant. Donors responded, many by increasing their initial level of commitment. Once the goal of $20 million was reached, negotiations began with the bank on how to manage the remaining $8.5 million. Allen had given faculty an early indication that something was in the works that would be truly transformational for the College. They believed her and waited to see exactly what this good news would be.

In April, two days before Allen was scheduled to report to the Board of Trustees on the successful completion of this endeavor, Fifth Third Bank pulled the rug from under her feet and, in effect, decided to end the College's institutional life. They revoked the deal they had negotiated for $20 million accompanied by a plan for extended payment of the remaining $8.5. Instead, they were willing to allow the pledges to expire and would require complete repayment of the entire $28.6 million. Since this was very unlikely, it seemed the bank was willing to let the College dissolve and take ownership of its property.

Allen was devastated. This "business decision" looked as though it was the end of the College's nearly 200-year history. She would be the first and last female president of the College. She would now have to face the prospect of unwinding the College and breaking the news to the community that Georgetown College was joining the ranks of colleges and universities that had been closing across the country.

Her remaining duty was to inform the donors that their commitments were no longer needed since the plan had collapsed. She called Robert Wilson first, since he had made the largest pledge. When Allen told him the news, he responded in a most unexpected way. In fact, his accountant had informed him recently that due to tax implications on some old investments, it would be a good idea to give some money away. "Well, forget the bank," he said. "I can do it." Wilson doubled his pledge to $16 million, enough to satisfy the total balance of the bonded debt. The College was saved from financial disaster.

The news of this remarkable gift and the successful plan to eliminate the debt was met with a tidal wave of acclaim and relief. Rosemary Allen, an English professor and Provost, with no fundraising experience at all, had accomplished what a string of previous presidents had been unable to do, thanks to the heartfelt commitment of Trustees, friends, and alumni. The accumulated debt burden that had hung around the College's neck for two decades was eliminated in one fell swoop.

Robert Wilson and President Allen celebrate the elimination of Georgetown College's debt with a ribbon cutting.

The public announcement was made on May 8, 2023, at a gathering on the steps of Giddings Hall. Students were heard expressing gratitude that now their children would be able to attend Georgetown College as most had been convinced its days were numbered. Faculty and staff rejoiced that their work was preserved, and for some of them, decades of service to the College had been redeemed from destruction. Not all the details were known at the time, but there was an overwhelming sense of pride and relief for Allen's action and for the College's supporters who had collaborated with great commitment to eliminate this existential threat to the College. The future now beckoned the College forward.

    The faculty organized a cook-out after graduation to thank President Allen for her heroic work. Daniel Graham laser printed 28 sticks with $1,000,000 to represent the debt. In a fire lit with a copy of the amended bond agreement with Fifth Third Bank, the sticks were built into a bonfire of debt relief. The smoke rising reflected the prayers of the faculty, staff, students, and the whole community of those who had served and loved the College throughout its long and storied history. The heat of the fire spoke to the energy and life still present in the community, and the celebration marked the true beginning of the next phase of the Georgetown College saga.

Chapter 17

The Mission: Christian Service and Love

By John Henkel

Georgetown College survives and thrives to the degree that its students, faculty, staff, and Trustees believe in its mission. Lacking the financial resources to make things easy, it often requires us to do something hard, and it rewards us with the sense that what we are doing is important and worthwhile. More than most places, Georgetown subsists on true believers, and especially on those who view its Christian identity as somehow central to its mission as a College. Yet this relationship has not always been clear, nor have different groups always agreed on what Georgetown College's Christian, and historically Baptist, identity should entail. This became an urgent question, especially after the split from the Kentucky Baptist Convention, when the College no longer had a denominational partner to anchor its identity and demonstrate its Christian bona fides. It was clear that the College could not abide the conservative turn that the KBC wanted in our instruction, but it was less clear how it would stay meaningfully Christian while pushing back against the anti-intellectualism and social conservatism that had come to dominate Baptist conventions throughout the South. Luckily, conversations about Georgetown College's Christian identity had been ongoing even before the KBC split in 2005; still, it took nearly 20 years for a consensus to emerge in the College's mission statement and other governing documents. In 2023, President Allen unveiled a new mission statement that explicitly defined the College's Christian identity as one "rooted in Christian love and service" and committed us to preparing students "to make a positive difference in the world." Remarkably, this new mission sits on the College website's "About" page alongside both a Christian identity statement that emphasizes "God's redeeming grace for all people and traditions" and a non-discrimination statement that includes "sex, sexual orientation, gender, [and] gender identity." As Provost Sands Wise puts it, "we're Christian and we mean it, and we're inclusive and we mean it." This combination makes Georgetown distinctive in the landscape of Christian higher education. It also defines a mission that many in the College community feel called to support, even when it's difficult. The gradual emergence of this mission is the story of this chapter.

As Georgetown College faces challenges—now as often in the past—the mission statement is its clearest and most public answer to those challenges. Often it is a new president who changes it, but sometimes exigent circumstances prompt the College to reconsider its mission and rearticulate it. So in 1912, during the last year of Arthur Yager's presidency, when Georgetown College was facing a drop in enrollment following the expansion of public higher education, he updated the "Character and Aim" section of the catalog to contrast Georgetown as a "standard Christian College of the highest type" with the public universities that were growing in Lexington, Richmond, and Bowling Green. The entire passage is notable for its emphasis on "the richness and usefulness of a life of intelligent Christian faith," but most notable is its opening preamble about the changing educational landscape:

> The educational life of America has been characterized by the development of a large variety of types of educational institutions. Each school must seek to find its place in the whole system and to fulfill its function there in such a way as to make its work indispensable. In the honest and efficient performance of its specific task, an institution of learning will merit and receive an ample patronage and adequate financial support.

President Yager left the College in 1913 to become governor of Puerto Rico, but this reflection on Georgetown's position and fortunes ran in the catalog through 1930 and speaks as clearly to the College's challenges today as it did in 1912. Just as then, Georgetown struggles with enrollment and growing competition from the public universities. And just as then, our fortunes depend on self-knowledge and the efficient performance of our specific task. If we know and believe in our mission, and if we fulfill our function in such a way as to make our work indispensable, then perhaps, as the 1912 catalog concludes, we may "confidently expect the patronage of those who prefer for their children this type of distinctly Christian education."

The Early Crouch Years: Guiding Principles and Discernment

What we would call the College's mission has historically been laid out in the first section of the College catalog, though not always succinctly or in a single section labeled "Mission." When Bill Crouch assumed the presidency in 1991, the catalog reflected the efforts and priorities of his predecessor, Morgan Patterson (1984–1991). Its introductory chapter—following the calendar and typical front matter—was called, "This is Georgetown," and opened with a long paragraph on "Our Role," describing the College in broad terms but emphasizing its character as a "private, coeducational liberal arts College, historically related to the Kentucky Baptist Convention." This was followed by a much briefer mission statement ("Purpose") that offered "opportunities for excellence in higher learning under Christian influences" and sought to balance the liberal arts with "a healthy interest in the professions." The heavy lifting of institutional commitments was handled through a list of 14 bullet points, which ranged widely from "foster a knowledge of and commitment to the Christian faith" to "provide quality support services and facilities." Next there came a relatively brief section on the College's history, followed by a paragraph on accreditation and affiliations and a longer section on the campus and its buildings. The size and relative importance of each of these sections changed over time, but the general shape of this opening section would persist well into the twenty-first century. Patterson's mission statement itself remained largely unchanged until 1998 and the bullet-point goals until 2014.

President Crouch's chief early contributions to the College's mission came from additions rather than alterations, and the first and most lasting of these was the introduction of his 8 Guiding Principles, which appeared on the opening pages of every catalog from 1992 through 2013. When Crouch arrived in 1991, the College had low morale but a sense that its academic quality was better than the public knew, so he wanted a statement of core values to help faculty and staff members align their efforts to grow the College's reputation and enrollment. The graphic below was published in the catalog, distributed to all faculty and staff, and posted in every classroom. Eventually the individual principles were hung on banners down Memorial Drive (now Robert N. Wilson Dr.).

8 GUIDING PRINCIPLES

QUALITY, *as expressed in Jesus Christ, is our way of life.*

EXCELLENT SERVICE *is our goal.*

LOYALTY *is our strength.*

TEAMWORK *is to be cherished.*

POSITIVE VISION *will motivate us.*

STEWARDSHIP *is our responsibility.*

PERSONAL GROWTH *will bring us joy.*

COMMITMENT *will be reaffirmed daily.*

The Guiding Principles served as a bedrock foundation to guide the Crouch administration's choices, especially as Baptist culture was rapidly changing with the rise of fundamentalism across the South. But for many in the faculty, they seemed more suited to a corporation than to a college and they failed to answer important questions about the College's identity. In particular, the role of Christianity at the College was only vaguely defined by treating Jesus as a model of quality. Questions about the College's Christianity were by no means unique to the Crouch years, but they grew more acute over his tenure, especially after the 2005 split from the Kentucky Baptist Convention.

The Mission: Christian Service and Love

Another notable feature of the early Crouch years was an increased emphasis on the College's history, which even took the traditional place of a mission statement in 1994 and 1995. For these two years, the Purpose statement and its bullet-point goals (still unchanged since Patterson) were relegated to the back of the introductory chapter—now titled, "Georgetown College... Yesterday and Today"—and an elegantly rewritten "History" section appeared front and center, emphasizing the College's long and venerable story while introducing its mission indirectly. Two facets of the College's character stand out after its founding. First is its liberal arts tradition, which it owes to the work of early president Howard Malcom (1840–1849):

> In his address to the student body and faculty in September, 1841, he described a broad-based curriculum, viewed ahead of its time compared to most American colleges. This new curriculum was designed to develop 'capacious views, solid judgment, self-command, right aims, conciliatory manners, genuine benevolence and pure morality.

The College's liberal arts tradition has often been a focus of its mission statements, but the other detail of this paragraph is more surprising: "Faculty and students labored together outside the classroom as joint building projects on campus and in the community resulted in the completion of Pawling Hall and Georgetown Baptist Church." These details were both drawn from Robert Snyder's ('53) *A History of Georgetown College* (1979), but their juxtaposition early in the catalog communicated not only that we were a Christian liberal arts College, but specifically that our understanding of that mission was tied to a sense of humility and service. Later, during the hard financial times of the post-Crouch era, this image of the faculty as humble co-workers was both inspiring and sometimes dispiriting, especially as faculty pay and benefits eroded.

Other than the 8 Guiding Principles, the most visible and influential statement of the College's mission was the Vision Statement that appeared first in the 1995 catalog and opened the intro chapter starting in 1996: "Georgetown College...an innovative community of scholars developing scholars committed to our heritage of Christian discernment." This short and memorable statement emerged from a faculty-driven process and was followed in the catalog by a paragraph elaborating on its key terms, "community," "innovative," "develop scholars," "heritage," "Christian," and "discernment." President Allen recalls it as a balanced, three-part commitment that put academics in the center, flanked by the important values of community and Christianity. And with only one small change—the addition of "ethical" in 1998 ("scholars developing ethical

English Professor Dr. Gwen Curry is an interpreter of Georgetown College's mission.

scholars")—this vision served the College well throughout President Crouch's tenure.

Perhaps the most notable thing about the new Vision Statement was the decision to anchor the College's Christian identity to the tradition of "Christian discernment" rather than to "Christian influences" or "Christian community," as earlier catalogs had, or to faith, as many other Christian Colleges were doing. During the eighties and nineties, there was a rising tide of fundamentalist anti-intellectualism in the Baptist world, which would eventually threaten academic freedom at Georgetown and lead to the College's separation from the Kentucky Baptist Convention in 2005. The College seems not only to have understood this threat, but to have met it head-on by claiming that free inquiry was itself an important Christian value: "Being Christian in content and manner allows us to freely pursue the truth, with clear *discernment* that all claims to possession of the truth by persons and groups should be subjected to the highest standards of inquiry" (emphasis original). In other contexts, faculty members have even gone so far as to claim that there is more academic freedom in a Christian College than in a secular public university. English professor Gwen Curry, who was CASE Kentucky Professor of the Year in 1993, spoke on "The Value of a Christian Education" to a group of Georgetown alumni at the 1994 meeting of the Kentucky Baptist Convention:

> I have heard people say that the phrase "Baptist higher education" is a contradiction of terms. These people hold some widespread misconceptions. They think that Christian education takes a "worksheet approach" to teaching—"here are the questions: here are the right answers." They think the teacher stands as the authority and tells the student all the answers.... [A]t Georgetown College I have never been told what to teach—or what not to teach. In freedom, by the light of my own Christian conscience, I select the books, the poems, the plays, the essays I teach in my English classes. I am freer teaching at Georgetown College, a Baptist College, than the teacher at a state school who is not allowed to discuss religion in the classroom.... Think. That is the key. The student at a truly Christian College is encouraged to think. Without fear.... Christ said, "You will know the truth, and the truth will set you free." Real Christian education is not afraid to examine all sides of an issue. It is not afraid to search for truth.[13]

Excerpts from Curry's speech were printed in the Spring 1995 Georgetown College alumni magazine and are worth reading at greater length. Her speech is roughly contemporaneous with the new Vision Statement and clearly shares its concern about anti-intellectualism in the church. Much of the College's future would be shaped by its dedication to the compatibility of religion and free inquiry.

The Georgetown College mission statement itself finally changed in 1997, roughly doubling in size. It was still mostly descriptive, but it could be longer because the Vision Statement was short and memorable.

> Georgetown College is a small, residential, co-educational liberal arts College distinguished by a combination of respected, rigorous undergraduate and graduate programs, an array of opportunities for involvement and leadership, a commitment to Christian values and its distinctive heritage. This provides an environment for intellectual, spiritual and social growth. Through a broad undergraduate program, the curriculum offers a foundation for shaping informed thought and action in order to prepare students for their place in society. Georgetown College seeks persons committed to supporting its mission and to realizing their full potential in this community of learners.

The paragraph, which was now labeled "Mission," made the point right away that Georgetown was a small liberal arts College, and then went on to emphasize strong academics, student life opportunities, Christianity, and its distinctive history. This was a period in which the College was doubling down on its academic strengths: it had started the Oxford Honors program in 1998 and had soon afterwards paid a London firm to develop an Oxford-style crest—with rampant tigers and a Latin motto borrowed from the University of Bristol (*vim promovet insitam,* "[learning] promotes ones innate strength")—which appeared on the catalog cover and was prominent in the College's branding from 1998 through 2014.

As Baptist fundamentalist movements grew in strength across the South, Georgetown College was staking its identity proudly to the Christian intellectual tradition and the compatibility of faith and reason. When President Crouch dedicated the new $16.5-million library in 1998, two quotes stood prominently on tall plaques on the building's facade. On the left was a quote that Religion professor Paul Redditt chose from the book of Proverbs: "Blessed is the person who listens to wisdom, for whoever finds wisdom finds life and receives favor from the Lord" (8:34a, 35). On the right was a quote that then-professor Rosemary Allen chose from John's Milton's *Areopagitica*: "Give me the liberty to know, to utter, and to argue freely according to conscience, above all liberties." Milton held a strong belief that the priesthood of the individual believer requires each of us to exercise his or her own reason in the practice of religion; he even held that one could be a heretic in the truth if he held right beliefs out of deference to authority instead of rational understanding. Religious freedom was equally important to early Baptist movements and had become central to many faculty members' understanding of Georgetown's Baptist heritage, especially since the Baptists who came to Kentucky had been a persecuted minority in Virginia. So when fundamentalists took over the Kentucky Baptist Convention and sought closer oversight of the College's religion and science curricula, the 2005 split was perhaps inevitable. The College's separation from the KBC posed a new and urgent challenge to its mission: how would the College define itself as a Christian institution now that it no longer had strong formal ties to the state Baptist convention?

Defining a Christian College

One traditional view of Christian higher education is that a good Christian College is academically largely the same as a good secular College, but its Christian faculty provides a better religious and moral influence outside the classroom. This has been the traditional view at Georgetown College, as seen in Patterson's mission statement, "opportunities for excellence in higher education under Christian influences," which appealed even to more conservative Baptists. But the rise of fundamentalism during the Crouch years strained the relationship between the College and the church: President Crouch worked hard to insulate a generally moderate faculty from a more conservative Board of Trustees, and the College's emphasis on discernment was partly an effort to protect academic freedom from the very same external pressures that would force its separation from the KBC in 2005. But while Crouch's strategy protected the College for a time from criticism that it wasn't Christian enough (or in the right ways), there was no central strategy to exert the College's Christian identity in other more authentic or palatable ways. So while some faculty were embracing a vision of Baptist Georgetown College rooted in individual religious and academic freedom, others—especially in the Philosophy and Religion departments—were talking about what a Christian College should be doing centrally and looking for ways to do more of those things. Eventually, the KBC breakup would force the College to define its Christian identity more clearly than it had done in the past; when this work began in earnest, it built largely on conversations and efforts centered on the third floor of Pawling Hall.

Christian higher education was a topic of debate both nationally and locally during the 1990s. Nationally, several scholars had written important books about the perceived incompatibilities between Christian commitments and the secular norms of the academy, and critiquing the sense among many that the project of Christian higher education was a lost cause.[14] During this time, a group of scholars and administrators at Baylor University were pushing back against the general trend of increasing secularization. Having survived a fundamentalist takeover attempt at the beginning of the decade, Baylor developed an ambitious plan to strengthen itself for the future by cultivating a world-class research faculty at the same time as leaning into—rather than away from—its Christian mission. Baylor 2012, as the campaign was called, took as its model Notre Dame, which was renowned for both its academic quality and its Catholic fidelity; the question was whether a Protestant university could do the same—especially a Baptist one. Baylor's resounding success was influential, not least on philosophy professor Roger Ward, who was an M.A. student there during the failed takeover and the early days of the movement that led to the campaign. Ward was the son of a Baptist minister and had first pursued the ministry himself before turning to philosophy, partly in reaction to the growing conservative movement among SBC churches and institutions. He had a deep affection for Baptist culture and its

The Mission: Christian Service and Love 147

democratic, egalitarian polity, but he couldn't abide the ascendancy of conservative fundamentalism across the South. So when he finished his Ph.D. and landed at Georgetown College in 1996—in a state where the conservatives had not yet taken over the state Baptist convention—he found himself among likeminded Baptists. But his experience at Baylor and his strong cultural ties to Baptist identity drew him toward a more activist approach to Georgetown's Christianity than many other faculty members. By Ward's own admission, he was puzzled by the College's Christian identity when he arrived—like many other faculty—and joined with other progressives in trying simply to escape the scrutiny of more conservative Baptists outside the College. But when he thought he perceived a general hostility to Baptists from some colleagues and administrators, his defensive hackles were raised and he started advocating to students and faculty alike for the integration of faith and learning and for more clarity about the value of a Baptist contribution to Christian higher education.

Ward had a strong sense of vocation to Baptist higher education, and through his efforts and with major support from the Lilly Endowment, vocation itself became a major theme in the way that Georgetown understood and expressed its Christian mission. Seeking to bolster Christian higher education against the narrative of its decline, Lilly sponsored a meeting in summer 1997 for scholars like Ward who had personal ties to the denomination that anchored their institution. Whether intentionally or not, they found themselves stewards of their church's educational tradition, and it emerged from this and a subsequent meeting that they all had a sense of calling to their work. These meetings were the Rhodes Consultation on the Future of Church-Related Colleges and they resulted in an anthology by their convener.[15] The Lilly grant that sponsored them also included $5,000 mini-grants for participants to convene similar meetings at their home institutions; so in Spring 1999, Ward gathered a dozen or so faculty—including Doc Birdwhistell, Norman Wirzba, Lydia Hoyle, Doug Griggs, Susan Bell, Homer White, and Dave Bowman, among others—to meet in the new library and talk about their sense of calling, both to their individual disciplines and to the work of the College. According to Ward, even the participants who were distant from their own faith traditions saw an element of providence in their coming to Georgetown and they were energized by seeing their roles and presence at Georgetown in the context of a greater purpose. As the Rhodes Consultation meetings proceeded across the country, vocation emerged as a galvanizing theme for the future of Christian higher education. So starting in the 1998-1999 school year, Lilly solicited grant applications for a program they called the Theological Exploration of Vocation Initiative. Working with Dean of the Chapel Dwight Moody, Ward applied for and won a $50,000 planning grant in 1999 and then a $2 million five-year grant covering 2000–2005, followed by a $500,000 extension grant for 2005–2008. These were years when Crouch's building program gave the appearance that the College was thriving (although it was accumulating debt); however, the Lilly grants funded significant real flourishing at the College in the early 2000s.

The Lilly Vocation money was initially administered by Dwight Moody, then later by Ward after Moody's departure from the College in 2009. Its benefits were widely felt and established a culture of "vocation and calling" language that touched much of the campus. For example, Lilly funded the first phase of Georgetown's career center, the Graves Center for Calling and Career. The grant also enabled Ward to expand the Christian Scholars Program from a modest scholarship to a comprehensive program, incorporating an annual Fall Break retreat, an academic vocation seminar, mission and service travel, and funding for student seminary visits. Since 2000, CSP has helped form hundreds of students to consider their calling. Perhaps more important is the Lilly grant's effect on College faculty, who would touch many times more students over course of their careers. The CSP program itself has been influential on various Philosophy and Religious faculty who have helped run it, including Sheila Klopfer, Jonathan Sands Wise, Derek Hatch, April Simpson, and Shelly Johnson. More broadly, Ward hosted annual conferences on topics like "Following the Call of the Church," which brought nationally recognized speakers like

The Mission: Christian Service and Love

Walter Brueggemann and Stephanie Paulsell to speak on campus and visit faculty members' classes. And each summer, Ward ran a faculty vocation seminar, which dozens of faculty members attended; some of these faculty members (myself included) were self-professed outsiders to the College's Christian mission who grew closer to it through Ward's persistent efforts. Beyond the campus, he used grant money to sponsor an annual "Young Scholars in the Baptist Academy" academic seminar at Regent's Park College, Oxford University, which nurtured the vocation of young Baptist scholars including Sheila Klopfer, Jonathan Sands Wise, Adam Glover ('07), and Derek Hatch (among many successful others); Baylor took over the program as the Baptist International Scholars Round Table in 2019. Even Student Life felt the impact of the Lilly grant, which paid for the high ropes course that James Koeppe ran as part of the Directions pre-College orientation retreat.

After the KBC split in 2005, the College had to show its Christian bona fides without the benefit of a denominational partner, so it was urgent now to adopt a central strategy for the College's Christian mission and to define more clearly what that mission was. President Crouch's most important step in this direction was hiring alum H. K. Kingkade ('83) to manage the College's relationship with Baptist churches. Kingkade advocated from early on for a formal statement of Georgetown's Christian identity and eventually worked with a faculty task force to develop the Christian Identity Statement, which was passed by the Trustees in April 2012 and appears in the 2012 catalog:

> Built on a Baptist foundation, Georgetown College pursues and cultivates a knowledge of and commitment to the Christian faith. Faculty, staff, and students are called to embrace their role in our community, which is characterized by God's redemptive grace for all people and traditions. Georgetown College promotes excellence as a means of discovering the truth about ourselves, our world, and God through the integration of mind, body, and spirit. Committed to faith in God, the College encourages all to discern their mission

and vocation in order to lead active and productive lives as exemplified in the teachings of Jesus Christ.

The statement emphasizes the College's Baptist roots and the importance of Christian faith, but it also—like the Trustee Bylaws it was based on—makes a point of inclusivity, specifying that God's redemptive grace is for "all people and traditions." The language about "excellence as a means of discovering the truth" faintly echoes the College's commitment to discernment during the mid-nineties, and the vocation language coincides with work that Ward had done with the Lilly grants since then. This Christian Identity Statement was palatable to the faculty because it was moderate and it persists unchanged on the College's website today. However, around the same time the College adopted it, the faculty was becoming more activist, both regarding its relationship with the administration and, in particular, about espousing a more vocally progressive understanding of its Christianity.

When Georgetown parted ways with the KBC in 2005, President Crouch and the Trustees were adamant that the College would remain a meaningfully Christian institution. But over the next decade there was less consensus about this point among the faculty because there was no consensus about what our Christian identity meant and entailed. Especially among younger and non-Baptist faculty, it was not well understood how moderate—even progressive—many of the College's institutional Baptists were. Nor could the College publicly acknowledge that it was less conservative than many Baptist churches, since this might hurt giving and recruiting. So, despite its recent work to define the Christian mission, the College found itself split during the Greene years over the nature of its Christianity. The major issue was inclusivity: could the College hire non-Christian faculty? and could it protect LGBTQ+ faculty and staff?

The Greene Years and the Challenge of Inclusivity

President Greene was a moderate Baptist, an institutionalist, and a capable administrator. From an institutional perspective, he was the right choice to continue and update Georgetown's traditional mission of free inquiry within a Christian culture that

The Mission: Christian Service and Love 151

is amenable to both conservatives and moderates. Although dire financial straits forced him to make drastic cuts to the faculty, his own scholarly background made him sensitive to faculty concerns, and he made a thorough and much-needed revision to the College's mission statement, drawing broadly on faculty and staff participation in the process. The result is a clear and relatively concise list of the College's strengths and priorities. But while Greene had personal sympathies with many progressive Christian positions—especially regarding women in the ministry, since his own daughter was ordained—he knew the College's bleak finances too well to risk alienating potential donors or students by moving too quickly on controversial issues. He, along with the Board of Trustees, served as a moderating and restraining influence on a faculty that was growing increasingly progressive since the College's separation from the KBC.

Of the two controversies that most shaped Georgetown's evolving sense of its Christian mission during the Greene years, one happened entirely before Greene's arrival on campus. Over the two years from 2010 to 2012, the faculty tried but failed to change the College's policy requiring that full-time tenure-track faculty be Christian. There was less consensus that this was necessary and appropriate following the KBC split, and it had always complicated the hiring process, especially in fields where Christians were scarce, like Asian languages. Moreover, the College had one Jewish professor, classicist Diane Arnson Svarlien, who was permanently barred from full-time tenure-track status by her religion. When Svarlien resigned in 2010 and was replaced by a full-time tenure-track hire (me), she, Melissa Scheier, and Homer White proposed that the College officially change its hiring policy. The question was referred to the Faculty Committee, where a research effort was led by Religion professor Sheila Klopfer. After reviewing the literature on Christian higher education and benchmarking 60 peer colleges and universities, the Subcommittee on Faculty Hiring proposed that the College allow the hiring of faculty who "contribute positively to the Christian identity of the College," provided that the administration develop policies to maintain a critical mass of Christian faculty who understand and support the College's

Baptist tradition.[16] In order for such a change to succeed, the subcommittee insisted that the College would also need to craft a clearer Christian Mission statement which "highlights the Christian intellectual tradition alongside its commitment to Christian values, virtues, and distinct heritage," and that this statement become a more central part of the College's identity. The subcommittee's work was concurrent with H. K. Kingkade's efforts to formulate the College's Christian Identity Statement; however, their report anticipates something much more ambitious and central to the College's true identity—a revision still needed today. Although the faculty passed the proposal (by a narrow margin), the Board of Trustees took no action and the proposal failed. On the one hand, this failure ensured that all full-time tenure-track faculty members would continue to be Christian; on the other hand, it sparked a principled debate about inclusivity, which would become a defining characteristic of Georgetown's distinctive Christian identity.

While changes to the College's Christian mission were happening slowly and organically, Greene's changes to the College's operational mission happened quickly and as part of a formal update to the strategic plan. As Greene explained in a memo, "the College has been functioning with extensive descriptor narratives, but these have largely lacked the necessary straightforwardness to state with precision the mission and essence of Georgetown College" (February 8, 2014). With the help of a Planning Council of faculty and staff, Greene revised both the mission statement and the strategic goals, which had persisted since 1987. The revised mission and goals opened the 2014 catalog, which also removed Crouch's 8 Guiding Principles.

The new mission kept the College's traditional view of Christian higher education as defined by excellent academics in a Christian environment, and it especially vaunted the College's "outstanding teaching and mentoring," which the faculty felt were under threat by ongoing force reductions. It also recognized the professions as full partner to the liberal arts and sciences, which other mission statements had stopped short of doing. Among the new strategic goals, many reflected traditional emphases like academic programs, the liberal arts core, and close

The Mission: Christian Service and Love 153

faculty-student bonds. But there is a notable change in the treatment of the College's Christianity: where before the College had sought broadly to "foster a knowledge of and commitment to the Christian faith," now its goal was specifically to nourish a faith that was inquisitive and intellectually resilient, and it specifically celebrated its Baptist heritage as an avenue through which it welcomed dissent. This was much more explicit than the brief mention of discernment in Crouch's vision statement. Free inquiry was at the heart of Georgetown's mission because it was at the heart of the Baptist identity, and there could be no reconciling with a state convention that thought otherwise.

The second controversy that shaped Georgetown's Christianity most decisively during the Greene years was the years-long fight for an LGBTQ+ non-discrimination policy; like the fight over the Christian hiring policy, this was an issue that started before Greene arrived on campus, but this one continued almost to the end of his tenure. In 2011, the College had hired a gay sociology professor, Sarah Cribbs, in full knowledge that she was gay; but it had no formal non-discrimination policy to protect LGBTQ+ employees from summary firing. Gay marriage was not yet legal nationwide, there were no federal or state non-discrimination protections, and at the time only three cities in Kentucky even had local protections; nor was the issue academic at the College, which had fired a gay staff member under external pressure in the past. The conservative objection to non-discrimination protections was that Christianity and homosexuality were mutually exclusive, but Cribbs and her wife were practicing Christians. Once again, the faculty took a principled stand to protect one of its own, many specifically out of their own sense of their Christian commitments. The effort to protect LGBTQ+ faculty and staff took years and had several phases. First, the Faculty Committee researched the issue and proposed a non-discrimination policy that passed the faculty by a wide margin in April 2012, but which the Trustees declined to ratify. Next, in the following academic year, a smaller group of faculty including Cribbs, Jen Price, Homer White, Eric and Yoli Carter, Nancy Lumpkin, and myself organized with students to protest the Board's inaction; in April 2013, they gave the Board a petition signed by 600 faculty, students, alumni, and community members, but again the Board declined to act. Over subsequent years, the group wrote letters and sponsored programming on campus arguing that Christianity was compatible with an LGBTQ+ identity; they affiliated with the Louisville-based Fairness Campaign to advocate politically for a citywide non-discrimination ordinance in Georgetown; and they worked with the community to organize an annual gay pride picnic starting in 2016. Gay marriage became legal nationwide in 2015, and Georgetown Fairness presented a proposed ordinance to the city council in 2017, at first unsuccessfully. The culture was changing, and the Board was quietly discussing the issue behind the scenes, out of view of the faculty, but with encouragement from Greene. Trustee Dr. Horace P. Hambrick was outspoken in his advocacy to other Board members. Hambrick had two gay children and felt strongly—as did many on the faculty—that Georgetown should welcome LGBTQ+ people because of its Christianity, not in spite of it. The Board adopted a new non-discrimination policy in 2018; the city passed an ordinance the following year. The length and difficulty of this fight meant that the inclusion of gay people was a major issue at Georgetown for seven years. Cribbs and her wife had moved on by the end, but Georgetown's Christian identity was now firmly anchored to inclusivity.

In other ways as well, Georgetown's Christianity grew in the direction of compassionate activism during the late Crouch years and the Greene years. Among the most notable examples are Regan Lookadoo's work against modern slavery and human trafficking, Susan Dummer's annual work with the Clothesline Project against sexual violence, Abraham Prades' more recent work with I Stand With Immigrants, and a Civil Rights field trip that Roger Ward and I have led since 2018. Through the Greene years, the College's Christian identity felt institutional—even conservative—and any kind of activism always felt a bit risky. But when Will Jones became president in 2019, he brought a different perspective. He was young, had two Black children, and his best friend was gay. For him it was obvious that Christianity should entail an activist concern for the rights of the marginalized. So, for all his flaws, Jones' unapologetic embrace of a more

The Mission: Christian Service and Love 155

progressive Christianity seemed to function as an institutional blessing for issues and efforts that the faculty already cared about. Short as it was, Will Jones' tenure marked the beginning of a more openly progressive character for the institution.

The Allen Years: Christian Love and Service

After years of struggle to preserve free inquiry against external pressures, the Greene years had been marked by a shift to internal struggle and dissension about what the central values of a Christian College should be. Academic freedom no longer seemed to be under threat, but it got clearer each year that the College's very survival was jeopardized by the lack of an agreed narrative about what made Georgetown College special. The College experienced two enrollment crises during the Greene and Allen years, both stemming from failures in leadership. The only successful VP for Enrollment Management in this period was former philosophy professor Jonathan Sands Wise, who was well-versed in Georgetown and Christian higher education, enabling him to develop his own marketing narrative about the College and its mission. Faculty activism was largely a thing of the past by the Allen years. COVID was hard, and by now the faculty knew the College's financial situation well enough to know that its future was outside of their control; they had also endured years of austerity and continuous belt tightening, without even a cost-of-living raise during the highest inflation in 40 years. The College's constituency had also changed starting in the Jones years due to the Legacy and Legends scholarship, which provided free tuition to many local students who might not have otherwise considered a Christian College. The cadre of so-called third-pillar students—who chose Georgetown for academic and/or religious reasons, not for sports or free tuition—shrank more and more over time. Not only was the College in financial peril, but there was a growing fear that Georgetown's distinctive brand of Christian liberal arts was no longer marketable, at least not without financial resources that we didn't yet have. Like many cultural institutions, free inquiry for its own sake had lost its momentum as an aspirational goal, seemingly replaced by narrow self-interest. So when President Allen revised the mission statement in 2023 to focus much more clearly on the College's Christian mission and the good our students would do in the world, she met the greatest non-financial challenge of the moment, helping students understand the good of Christian higher education and helping faculty all row in the same direction with an updated shared narrative.

President Allen's mission statement reflects the evolving self-image of the College, and in one sense, it was truly a group effort, but the actual work of composing and revising fell on Allen herself and on her cabinet. Influential in this group was Jonathan Sands Wise, whom Allen appointed Provost when she was named President. Sands Wise had long promoted a vision of Christian love and service because he was a virtue ethicist, who believed that our faith—like any sincere belief—must lead us to concrete actions. He was at Baylor University for graduate school during the controversial campaign to make it more Christian, and he shared the sentiment that faith should be broadly integrated into the life of a Christian College. This was somewhat in tension with the traditional view that academics and faith were separate concerns; but the College had long been leaning toward a more integrated faith, especially as it found its footing in a more progressive Christianity. Sands Wise had also worked in Admissions, which gave him a clear focus on the new mission's marketability. After teaching for six years on the tenure track, he had been laid off in the Greene-era faculty reduction, then moved to Academic Success and later, surprisingly, made VP for Enrollment Management. He had no experience in Admissions, but he had demonstrated strong leadership as Associate Dean of Academic Success, and Greene needed a true believer—someone who understood Georgetown and could authentically convey why students should choose Georgetown College. When Sands Wise arrived in Admissions, they were downplaying the College's Christian identity; he reversed this trend, but it was largely up to him to decide what to emphasize, since the Greene-era mission statement wasn't designed for marketing. His focus on Christianity as the driving force behind a life of service is evident in the "GC Means" brochure that admissions counselors began distributing on the road starting in 2017: "GC Means Christian

The Mission: Christian Service and Love   157

and Caring." The brochure unfolds into a cross, with a two-fold spread featuring the Chapel and explaining that GC is not just a "Christian institution" [scare quotes original], but an "ever-caring, always welcoming, Christ-serving College" where "[w]e strive to live out the Christian virtues of Faith, Hope, and Love in everything we do."

Allen herself arrived at Christian love and service by a different route, shaped partly by her own initial experience as an outsider, since she was both a non-Baptist (Episcopal) and a woman working in a denomination skeptical of women in power. In her academic training as a Miltonist, Allen had read Puritan theologians and Renaissance literature that used rebellious women as a proxy for religious defiance of the king; despite the general imperative for women to obey, the religious freedom specifically of women became a test case for the supremacy of the individual believer's conscience. When she first arrived at Georgetown, Allen was hesitant about its religious mission because she didn't know Baptist culture; and her unease being a woman here was reinforced by a constant stream of English composition papers arguing whether women should be allowed in the clergy. It took her about a year to find her footing, which she did in conversation with English colleagues Steve May and Gwen Curry. Curry, by contrast with Allen, was the consummate insider—a Baptist and the daughter of a Georgetown professor—but she was also a feminist, and for her it was the Baptist tradition of intellectual and religious freedom that helped her reconcile the contraries that Allen was struggling with. Like Curry, Allen in the 1990s and 2000s saw the tradition of Christian discernment as central to Georgetown's character as both a Christian and a liberal arts College. Allen also clearly valued activist love and compassion, and she helped students start an alternative newspaper, *Flipside*, when the administration barred a gay student from publishing in the *Georgetonian* in the mid-1990s. When Allen served as Provost under Crouch and Greene, the College took a big-tent approach to its Christianity, trying to make space for conservatives and moderate/progressives alike. But in its unwillingness to be decisive about a controversial social issue like gay inclusion, it was really catering only to conservatives—and without much success. After she became President, Allen's thinking about the College and its mission was influenced most of all by the Danford Thomas lecture given by Linda Livingstone, President of Baylor ("Why the World Needs Christian Higher Education," March 21, 2023). Livingstone spoke passionately about the importance of faith as the cornerstone of Baylor's mission and of her own presidency. Allen was struck by the effectiveness of having a shared sense of what was most important in Christianity but she knew that the cornerstone of Georgetown's mission couldn't be only faith, since an overconfident faith led too often to dogmatism and an ease of judging others. It was a dogmatic faith that led the fundamentalists to threaten academic freedom in the 1990s and 2000s, and today the same dogmatic faith is leading to culture wars over issues like gay rights, threatening the moral freedom in a similar way. Ironically, an emphasis primarily on faith tended in practice to threaten the freedom of conscience at the center of Georgetown's Baptist heritage. To preserve this freedom—and the tradition of discernment the College vaunted in earlier years—Allen felt that the College's mission would have to focus on what a Christian should do, not just what he or she should believe. And its recent history had an authentic answer to that question: love and serve.

Following a whole-faculty retreat, more than one survey, and much revision by the cabinet and especially by Allen herself, Allen's new mission statement debuted in draft form in May 2023 and was approved by the Board of Trustees later that summer, along with the rest of the strategic plan.

> Georgetown College's mission is to provide a welcoming and challenging educational community, rooted in Christian love and service, that prepares students to make a positive difference in the world.

Allen had insisted on its shape: it would say explicitly what it was ("Georgetown College's mission is...."), it would be concise—so that you could memorize it—and it would be aspirational, saying what we try to do but don't yet do fully. She regarded it not as a break from the past but as a continuation and refinement of

The Mission: Christian Service and Love

President Greene's mission. But its difference from the preceding missions is unmistakable, and not just in its striking brevity. Other mission statements have been essentially descriptions—if aspirational ones—while this one is an agenda. It is also much more explicit: it no longer takes for granted a shared understanding of Christianity nor assumes the value of a liberal arts education. As Christians, we are called to love and serve; and when we teach, our explicit goal is that our students go from here to love and serve in turn, and that they make the world a better place for doing so. The May 2023 draft also included strategic goals, complete with bullet points organized under relevant headings: to be welcoming, to be challenging, to be an educational community, to embody Christian love, to embody service, and to make a positive difference in the world. These bullet points were never finished or formally approved, but it bears noting that the draft section on Christian love makes two points, which correspond to the two major themes of Georgetown's Christianity over the last 35 years.

- We will endeavor to demonstrate unselfish, benevolent, unconditional care for all members of our community.
- We will encourage a faith that seeks understanding through free and thoughtful inquiry.

For Allen and for Georgetown College, Christianity means love, which commits us to inclusion and entails a culture of confident free inquiry, without fear or constraint. As Gwen Curry said, "Real Christian education is not afraid to examine all sides of an issue. It is not afraid to search for truth."

When early Baptists came over the mountains into Kentucky, they were a religious minority fleeing persecution in Virginia. They had an absolute commitment to religious freedom and the autonomy of each person to read and interpret the Bible for themselves; this latter commitment entailed the need for an educated clergy, which in time gave rise to Georgetown College. But when Southern Baptists became a religious majority in the twentieth century, this commitment to freedom and autonomy gave way to purity tests like the confrontation over Georgetown's curriculum, or the more recent expulsion of churches with female pastors. The recent history of Georgetown College's mission has been one of fidelity to historical Baptist principles of freedom and religious autonomy for each community. When we split from the KBC, when we affirmed our inclusivity, and as we continue to support female students in their call to ministry, we have made these decisions guided by our own Christian consciences, shaped by years of reading, prayer, and even argument. As a Christian college, we promote a culture of free inquiry without fear because we believe that reason, which is also from God, will not undermine our faith. And we open our community in loving hospitality to all because we believe in the equality and innate dignity of all God's children. Discernment and inclusion are the foundation of Georgetown's mission of Christian love and service. And in humble service, we pray that we can help our students find their calling to better the world through their lives. Our students today know, even if they can't say it yet, that dreaming only of personal success or material comfort is narrower than they deserve—or than the world deserves from them. They want larger meaning in a world that has narrowed its sights. Georgetown is just the kind of school to meet this challenge. We know our mission, so now we must fulfill it in a way that makes our work indispensable. We face real challenges, particularly in terms of resources and morale, but I always return to the image of the faculty as humble co-laborers in building Pawling Hall: our efforts are hard, but with a shared sense of purpose, we can at least pray that we are building something lasting and worthwhile.

Epilogue

The Road Leads Ever Onward

The story of Georgetown College and its resilience through the events of the last 30 years is more than a list of names, dates, and actions. Leadership in various forms emerged in special times of need and direction. The College was founded to extend the witness of the saving power of God through education. In all its permutations in the events recorded here, that witness has stayed true. The changes of leadership, relationship with its sponsoring denomination, and its financial condition reflect this continuing and focusing purpose. Georgetown College remains a place sustained by the Christian hope of redemption, a place of dedicated service to God, expressed through an institution of higher learning. Underlying this hope and dedication is the grace of God that draws together students, families, faculty, staff, Trustees, and a supportive community.

Challenges continue for Georgetown College. Enrollment still lags behind expectations, the operating budget remains unbalanced, and new programs have been further postponed due to SACSCOC placing the College on probation in December 2024, despite the extraordinary change to its asset balance sheet. The disappointment at this news was tempered by the explanation that the action was "for good cause," which in their terms means confidence that Georgetown can address the problems in short order. The tasks required to do this are clear, and the goals are achievable.

This raises fundamental questions that will mark the College's future. What is the good we are seeking together? What is the role of a Christian and Baptist College in this third decade of the twenty-first century, within the state of Kentucky and in our country? What future will the College be entering when it celebrates its bicentennial in 2029? And who will lead us into that next century of life as a college?

The answers, of course, will be made by living the questions authentically and hopefully. Georgetown College's community needs students educated in technical fields like physical science, medicine and business, and in helping fields like ministry, education, psychology, the arts, and philosophy. These students

The Georgetown College sign welcomes all to the college crescent and Giddings Hall.

need a place like Georgetown College, where they can expand their horizons to understand the world's needs and their responsibilities in meeting these needs through service and care. In addition, the community of academic institutions needs Georgetown College as a symbol of its historic faithfulness to a religious tradition and community, but also as a witness to the ways faithfulness commends new and courageous approaches to the physical and spiritual needs of the times.

The Christian mission of Georgetown College has never been more important for its community, to "provide a welcoming and challenging educational community, rooted in Christian love and service, that prepares students to make a positive difference in the world." On the road to fulfilling this mission the College will continue to raise the vision of its members and surrounding community that, with God's grace, all things are possible.

Appendix

The Seal of Georgetown College

The Georgetown College website explains that on the *Sigillum Collegii Georgetonensis*, or "Seal of Georgetown College," the motto *Respice Finem* may be translated to "Consider (or reflect on) the goal." The Book represents the search for knowledge. The Cross indicates the fact that Christ and Christian faith are both the foundation and purpose behind the institution. The Greek Building represents culture. The Crown represents a perfectly balanced combination of learning, culture, and religion, which carries its own reward of success. The Sun represents the dawn of a golden age for which humanity has always striven and which is one of the goals of human endeavor.

Appendix

The Seal of Georgetown College

Endnotes

[1] Robert Snyder, *A History of Georgetown College* (Georgetown, KY: Georgetown College, 1979), 141.

[2] Ibid., 155.

[3] Ibid., 153.

[4] Ibid., 178.

[5] James Duane Bolin, *Kentucky Baptists, 1925-2000: A Story of Cooperation*, (Brentwood, TN: Baptist History and Heritage Society; Nashville, TN: Fields Publishing, 2000), 263.

[6] The statistics and trends presented in this chapter are based on available data, which is sometimes incomplete. This may affect the accuracy of the conclusions. Quotations are from the College catalogs of the era.

[7] Kenny Davis tells the story of the controversial Olympic game in *Better than Gold* (Sikeston, MO: Acclaim Press, 2014).

[8] Dwight A. Moody, *It's About Time: A Memoir of Ministry at Georgetown College* (Bloomington, IN: IUniverse, 2010), 43.

[9] This description of the College's relationship to the Kentucky Baptist Convention appears in each of the Audited Financial Statements for Georgetown College from 1995 to 2006. It serves as a preamble to the amount of "unrestricted revenue from the Convention" the College received that year.

[10] The issue would remain at an impasse until 2018 when the Trustees adopted a non-discrimination policy advocated by Trustee Dr. Horace Porter Hambrick.

11 The task of guiding the faculty through this arduous process was entrusted to a General Education Revision Committee composed of Barbara Burch (English), Juilee Decker (Art), Doug Griggs (Education), Brad Hadaway (Philosophy), and co-chairs Bill Stevens (Biology) and Cliff Wargelin (History).

They translated ideas into models and chaired sub-committees that emerged to flesh out key aspects of the new program.

[12] "Georgetown College gets 'clean bill of health,'" *Baptist Standard* (January 23, 2006), 14.

[13] Gwen Curry, "The Value of a Christian Education," *Insights*, 23:3 (Spring 1995), 10-11.

[14] See, for example, Mark Schwehn, *Exiles from Eden: Religion and the Academic Vocation in America* (Oxford: Oxford University Press, 1992), George M. Marsden, *The Outrageous Idea of Christian Scholarship* (Oxford: Oxford University Press, 1998), and James Tunstead Burtchaell, *The Dying of the Light: The Disengagement of Colleges and Universities from their Christian Churches* (Grand Rapids, MI: Wm. B. Eerdmans, 1998).

[15] Stephen R. Haynes, ed., *Professing in the Postmodern Academy: Faculty and the Future of Church-Related Colleges* (Waco, TX: Baylor University Press, 2002).

[16] "Final Recommendations and Findings of the Subcommittee on Faculty Hiring" (March 30, 2012). See also "Research Collected and Compiled by the Subcommittee on Faculty Hiring (April 2010–March 2012): Faculty Hiring as it Relates to the Christian Mission of Georgetown College" (March 30, 2012).

Index of Names

Aikin, Carter, xiii

Allen, Rosemary, xiii, xvii, xviii-xix, 16, 21, 48, 102-104, 109, 113, 120, 122, 125-136, 137, 142, 145, 155-159

Apple, Lindsey, 16

Ballard, Michelle, 67

Baeza, Jose, 67

Barber, Robbi, 64, 114

Beard, Sylvia, 16

Bell, Susan, 147

Berry, Wendell, 68, 114

Birdwhistell, Ira J. ('Doc'), 6, 8-9, 147

Birdwhistell, Mary Alice, 67

Bisese, Ann Leigh, 29

Bisese, Steve, 27-29, 38

Bowman, Dave, 147

Bratcher, Robert, 48

Bratcher, Winnie, 65

Briggs, Christopher, 74

Brown, James Graham, 14

Brush, Bob, 32

Budge, Jen, 77

Buhr, Neely Thomas, 33

Burch, Barbara, 167

Burtchaell, James Tunstead, 47

Bush, George H. W., 29, 38

Cairo, Michael, 82

Callahan, Darryl, 75

Carter, Eric, 153

Carter, Yoli, 153

Cawthorne, Chris Kerr, 15

Cawthorne, Don, 15

Chitwood, Paul, 107

Christensen, Mark, 82

Clark, Lloyd, 29

Coble, Chris, 110

Coke, Todd, 122

Colley, Scott, 125

Collins, Martha Layne, 75, 87-88

Cook, Steve, 42, 58

Cooper, John Sherman, 5

Cordell, James, 7

Crace, Ben, 8

Craig, Elijah, 11, 108

Crawford, Tara Jo (Sword), 66

Crouch, William H., Sr., 42

Crouch William H, Jr., xiv, xvii-xviii, 1-2, 4, 7-9, 12-13, 16, 27-29, 31-32, 35-39, 42-45, 50, 51-53, 56, 59, 63-64, 75, 77, 82, 85, 88, 91-94, 97-99, 101, 103, 105, 108, 121-22, 123, 126-28, 130, 139-42, 144-46, 148-50, 152-54, 157

Crouch, Jan, 98, 121-22

Cronin, Bill, 32-33

Cubbage, Carolyn Hale, 30

Cunningham, David S., xiii

Curry, Gwen, 125, 142-53, 157, 159, 168

Czarnecki, Kristin, 79

Davis, Bob, 30-31

Davis, John, 129, 132

Davis, Kenny, 31, 167

Decker, Juilee, 167

Donley, Kevin, 32

Dudgeon, Hollis, 114

Dummer, Susan, 154

Earwood, Greg, 65

Eddleman, H. Leo, 3-5, 110

Eden, Marsha (Oakes), 115

Edwards, Scottie, 31

Elder, Charlotte (Stickle), 115

Ellers, Frank, 125

Elrod, Ben M., 3, 5, 35

Enlow, Eugene, 69

Evans, Brian, 64, 73-74, 111

Eviston, Eddie, 33

Felton, Sharon, 9, 69

Fiddes, Paul, 68

Figg, Douglas, 119

Fitzpatrick, Scott,, 115

Flores, Theresa, 83

Fox, Robert, 58

Fruge, Eric, xiv, 42-44, 46, 58, 68, 86

Index of Proper Names

Fryman, Jo Anna, xiii

Fuller, Melodie, 27, 28, 35

Gambill, Todd, 29, 71-73, 75, 111

Gillespie, Bill, 37

Glover, Adam, 149

Goode, Earl, Jr., xiv, xvii, 52, 89, 93-94, 106, 122

Graham, Daniel, 115, 136

Graves, Douglas, 15

Greene, Carolyn, 106-07, 115, 117

Greene, M. Dwaine, xiv, xviii-xix, 102, 104, 105-16, 117, 128-31, 150-57, 159

Gregory, Joel, 64

Griffith, Timothy, 82

Griggs, Douglas, 15-16, 147, 167

Hadaway, Bradford, 78, 79, 167

Hambrick, Horace Porter, 119, 154, 167

Hanly, J. P., 109

Hatch, Derek, 148, 149

Hawkins, Bert, 27

Hawkins, Donna, 33

Henkel, John, xiii, 151

Holden, Ken, 69

Honeycutt, Roy, 41

Houston, William 'B. I.', 93

Hoyle, Lydia, 6-7, 147

Hoyle, Rick, 6

Insko, Cynthia, 66-67

Jenkins, Philip, 114

Johnson, Andi, 33

Johnson, Johnnie, 59, 87

Johnson, Laura, 73, 111

Johnson, Shelly, 148

Johnson, Susan, 33, 74

Johnson, Wayne, 7

Jones, William "Will", xviii-xix, 102, 104, 117-24, 130-31, 154-55

Kiernan, Jean, 60

Kindrick, Garvel, xiv, 87, 126

Kingkade, H. K., 53, 58, 60-62, 66, 149, 152

Klopfer, Sheila, xiv, 7, 68, 80-81, 93, 148-49, 151

Koeppe, James, 28, 72, 109, 149

Kopp, Rick, 82

Kruschwitz, Robert, xiv, 16

Lacy, Jimmy, 66

Lancaster, Harry, 31

Langdon, Bethany Hornback, 132, 134

Langlands, Bryan, 66-67, 113

Lewis, Joe, 6

Lindsay, Dwight M., 14

Livingston, Tracy, 82

Livingstone, Linda, 158

Lohman, Gretchen, 28-29, 109

Lookadoo, Regan, 60, 83, 154

Lopez, Alexandria (Smiley), 120

Lucas, Charlene, 28

Lunceford, Joe, 6

Lynch, Michelle, 91, 112, 129

Malcom, Howard, 141

Mallow, Vernon, 6

Manning, John Walker, 16

Marshall, Alice (Gardner), 9-10

Marshall, Bill, 9-10

Marshall, Ed, 29

Marshall, Molly, 68

Mason, Frank, 86

Mason, Meda (Banks), xiv

Mason, Tiera, 120

May, Steve, 125, 157

McCarthy, Emily, xiv

McCloskey, Andrea, 74

McKenzie, Karyn, xiii, 2, 17, 93

Miller, Dan, 75, 85, 87

Miller, Timothy, 8

Mills, Robert L. Sr., 3-5, 110

Mills, Robert L. Jr., xiv, 130-31

Milton, John, 145

Moak, James, 85-86, 126, 128

Mohler, Albert, 41, 43

Moody, Dwight A., 10, 65, 68, 148

Moore, Wayne, 42

Newbery, Ilse, 15

Newman, Elizabeth, 68

Nicholson, John, 77

Noe, Andrew, 114

Oakley, Jerry, 44

Oldham, Robin, xiv, 110-11

Index of Proper Names

Osborne, Happy, 30-32, 74-75

Owsley, Laura, xiv, 28, 115

Palmer, Parker, 15

Pardue, Howard, 32

Patterson, W. Morgan, 1, 11, 35, 39, 125, 128, 139, 141, 145

Paulsell, Stephanie, 68, 114, 149

Penn, Frank, 103, 133

Perkins, Beth (Stricker), 8, 65

Perkins, Kenneth, 8, 65

Pollard, William, 126

Prades, Abraham, 154

Price, Jennifer, 73, 79, 153

Price, Marcus, 67

Pryor, Martha Chatham, 114

Puglisi, Michael, 19

Rasberry, Todd, 108, 110, 129

Redding, George Walker, 68

Redditt, Alan, xiv, 46

Redditt, Megan (Williams), 29, 71

Redditt, Paul, 6-7, 145

Reese, Fenton, 88

Reid, Jim, 30-31

Rich, Michael, 60

Rogers, Judy, 13, 75

Ruden, Sarah, 68, 114

Rupp, Adolph, 31

Salyer, Rachel Vincent, 33

Sampson, Will, 60

Sands Wise, Jonathan, xiii, 104, 109, 112-13, 120, 122, 129, 132, 138, 148-49, 155-56

Scheier, Melissa, 82, 151

Schimmoeller, Christina, 18, 33

Schimmoeller, Trina, 33

Schweickhardt, Sean, 66

Simpson, April, 148

Singer, Rebecca, 120

Somerville, Jim, 65

Smith, Edward (Ed), xiii

Smith, Diane Graves, 15

Smith, Larry, 77

Snider, Jason, 120

Snyder, Robert, 141, 147

Stafford, Marjorie Bauer, 14-15

Stevens, William, 82, 167

Stevenson, Bryan, 114

Stowe, Emily, 109

Stubbs, Leah, xiii

Svarlien, Diane Arnson, 61, 151

Taul, Glenn, 108

Thayer, Damon, 77

Tilford, Danny, 7

True, Guthrie, xiv, 44

VanHoose, Richard, 5

Volf, Miroslav, 68, 114

Ward, Eric, 73

Ward, Roger, xi, 10, 48, 68, 93, 114, 146-50, 154

Wargelin, Cliff, 167

White, Homer, 93, 147, 151, 153

Willimon, Will, 68, 114

Wilson, Anne Wright, 36, 38

Wilson, Robert N., 36, 103, 134-35, 140

Wiseman, Frank, 15

Wirzba, Norman, 114, 147

Wolterstorff, Nicholas, 68

Woods, Justin, 8

Wyatt, Macy, xiv, 28

Yager, Arthur, 138

York, Hershael, xiv, xviii, 42-43, 45

About the Author

Roger Ward joined the faculty of Georgetown College in 1996 following his Ph.D. from the Pennsylvania State University. His academic interests include American philosophy and the philosophy of religion. In addition to authoring several books and essays on philosophy, he is the editor of the *Pluralist*, the journal for the Society for the Advancement of American Philosophy. Ward is the founding director of the Center for Christian Discernment and Academic Leadership at the College. He and his wife Elaine reside in Georgetown, KY.

About the Author

www.ingramcontent.com/pod-product-compliance
Lightning Source LLC
Chambersburg PA
CBHW072130160426
43197CB00012B/2060